The Self-Care Handbook

The Self-Care Handbook

Connect with yourself and boost your wellbeing

Gill Hasson

CAPSTONE
A Wiley Brand

This edition first published 2020

© 2020 Gill Hasson.

Registered office

John Wiley & Sons Ltd, The Atrium, Southern Gate, Chichester, West Sussex, PO19 8SQ, United Kingdom

For details of our global editorial offices, for customer services and for information about how to apply for permission to reuse the copyright material in this book please see our website at www.wiley.com.

Wiley publishes in a variety of print and electronic formats and by print-on-demand. Some material included with standard print versions of this book may not be included in e-books or in print-on-demand. If this book refers to media such as a CD or DVD that is not included in the version you purchased, you may download this material at http://booksupport.wiley.com. For more information about Wiley products, visit www.wiley.com.

Designations used by companies to distinguish their products are often claimed as trademarks. All brand names and product names used in this book are trade names, service marks, trademarks or registered trademarks of their respective owners. The publisher is not associated with any product or vendor mentioned in this book.

Library of Congress Cataloging-in-Publication Data is Available:

ISBN 978-0-857-08812-3 (hardback)
ISBN 978-0-857-08816-1 (ePDF)
ISBN 978-0-857-08815-4 (epub)

Cover Design: Wiley
Cover Image: © Anna Paff/Shutterstock

Set in 12/15pt, SabonLTStd by SPi Global, Chennai, India.

Printed in the UK by Bell & Bain Ltd, Glasgow

10 9 8 7 6 5 4 3 2 1

Bet; you knew how to take good care of yourself! X

Contents

Contents

Introduction

My mother always says people should be able to take care of themselves, even if they're rich and important.
                                        Frances Hodgson Burnett

Who needs self-care? You do. We all do. Self-care is central to living a life that makes us feel good and that we feel good about. And yet too few of us recognize and honour our need to balance our mind and body; to protect, maintain, and improve our physical and mental health and our wellbeing.

The NHS's website 'One You' www.nhs.uk/oneyou says that 'without knowing it, by the time we reach our 40s and 50s many of us will have dramatically increased our chances of becoming ill later in life. Whether we are eating the wrong things, drinking more than we should, continuing to smoke despite everything we know, or just not being active enough, all of these small things can add up to an unhealthy you. But, it's not always easy to make a change in our busy lives – tempting treats in easy reach, bigger portions for everything we eat, and technology that allows us to shop, stay in touch, and be entertained without ever having to leave the sofa. Modern life is ganging up on us'.

The good news is that you *can* do something about it. This book helps you discover how simple, straightforward changes can add up to making a positive difference that leads to a happier, healthier, more fulfilling life, not just in the future, but starting right now.

You deserve a happy, healthy fulfilling life. Don't you? The first chapter of this book explains that self-care isn't selfish. Quite the contrary. Self-care is self-respect. To convince you of this, in Part I, Chapters 2 and 3 help you to get into a self-care mindset – a positive mindset – to recognize that whatever your faults and failings, you're as good as anyone else; that you're worth taking care of and that you deserve to feel good about yourself.

The rest of Part I explains why and how to take care of your mental health; how to manage and reduce stress and 'overwhelm' in your personal and work life. It also includes advice about managing your finances. You might not think that money has anything to do with mental health, but although money is *not* the root of all evil, no matter how much or how little you've got, it *is* one of life's biggest stressors.

Part II of this book moves on to taking care of your body. Eating well, exercising regularly, and getting enough sleep are touchstones of self-care and can keep you healthy, fit, and resilient.

But whether it's self-care for your mind or your body – even when you know that self-care is important – it can be hard to make it happen; make it a normal part of your days and weeks and a normal part of your life.

Self-care isn't just about doing the 'right' thing, though; it's about making changes to fit *your* life. The aim of this book is to help you work out ways that you can do this. In each chapter, I explain why you need self-care in that specific area of your life, acknowledge the barriers and challenges, but then offer ways you can apply self-care actions into your life.

Self-care *does* take some effort, be it planning and preparing healthy meals, finding ways to be physically active, or letting go of your day to get to bed on time. Even finding time to do enjoyable things requires effort on your part too! You just need to take small steps; choose one or two things – one or two changes – at a time, that you really think you can do, focus on them and make them a habit. Then move onto the next thing.

✻ ✻ ✻ ✻ ✻ ✻ ✻

'Self-care' may be the new buzz word – but 'self-help' isn't. It's what I write and teach about. In this book I've included writing from some of my other books, in particular from three of my recent books: *Declutter Your Life*, *Kindness*, and *Happiness*.

In fact, this book brings together so much of what – through my teaching, coaching, and writing – I encourage others to try and do: to accept themselves, to work on their self-esteem, to manage overwhelm at work and in their personal lives, to let go of people that are draining them, and seek out and spend time with positive people and do enjoyable things. And, to eat well, get moving, and get outside more. (I'm a walker; I'm regularly out walking in the Sussex countryside with family and friends and I'm also a trained walk leader – I lead walking holidays in Europe several times a year.)

Whether you've done very little to take care of yourself, or you've let self-care slide beneath your feet; if, like the Mad Hatter told Alice 'You used to be much more … "muchier." You've lost your muchness', then this book – *The Self-Care Handbook* will help you regain your muchness and become 'more muchier'.

Read on!

1
What and Why Self-Care?

What's self-care? It's taking care of yourself. It's looking after yourself. Self-care is health care; care of your mental health and physical health.

In the UK, the Self Care Forum www.selfcareforum.org defines self-care as: 'The actions that individuals take for themselves, on behalf of and with others in order to develop, protect, maintain and improve their health, wellbeing or wellness.' And according to the Royal Australasian College of Physicians, self-care involves 'looking after your needs, on a daily basis and in times of crisis in order to maintain a positive emotional, psychological and physiological resilience and wellbeing'.

Self-care involves being aware of and being connected to yourself; it involves knowing what you need to do and not do to ensure your wellbeing. It's taking responsibility for yourself; for your mental, emotional, physical wellbeing. It's knowing that *not* looking after yourself can have a detrimental effect on your health, welfare, or happiness.

Self-care isn't something you do once and tick off the list. It's the ongoing practice of keeping yourself physically and emotionally healthy. It should be a normal part of your life, how you live your life; who you are and what you do.

Speaking in 2018 about Self Care Week – an annual UK national awareness week – Dr Pete Smith, co-chair of Self Care Forum, said: 'Our aim is to embed it (self-care) into everyone's everyday life making it a life-long habit and culture. We want people to instinctively understand how to look after their own physical health and mental wellbeing. Self-care is nothing less than actions that lead to a happier, healthier, more fulfilling life.'

Determining what, when, and how much self-care you need is found in being aware of and understanding what your needs *are* at any one time. If, for example, your life is so full right now that you're feeling overwhelmed, then self-care may mean finding ways to manage this period of your life. It may mean bringing a slower pace, rest, and reflection into your life. If your life currently feels low and flat, or empty, then activities that bring you greater connection to others and the world around you may be what you need.

For some people, self-care might mean managing an acute or chronic illness or disability. For others, it could be about creating a healthy work–life balance. It might mean being more physically active or maintaining or switching to more healthy eating. For some of us, self-care might mean prioritizing a morning or evening walk, making time to write a daily reflective journal, or having time out to read a novel. It could mean a weekly dance class or learning to ride a motorbike. Whatever helps you feel physically and mentally on top of things is all part of self-care.

Knowing Yourself

Throughout your life *you* are the one constant. You're the only person in the world that you'll always have a relationship with. Self-care is not just about 'me', it's about 'me too'. Self-care reflects a belief in your own, innate worth; it's about taking care of yourself as you would someone you love, with the same respect, consideration and concern, care and compassion.

Self-care is knowing how you feel and what you need without being neurotic – overly anxious and obsessed – about it. It's about knowing what's happened, what's happening, and what you've got coming up and making positive, helpful choices as a result of that knowledge; making choices that are right for you.

Self-care involves learning what does and doesn't work for you, under different circumstances – when life is just rolling along or when life is difficult and challenging – so that you can create and establish routines and habits which together protect and maintain, develop and improve your health and wellbeing.

If you're not already taking good care of yourself, self-care means shaking things up and doing things differently, especially if you experience the sort of issues on the list below. Which of these do you regularly experience?

- Being tired.
- Feeling sluggish.
- Feeling overwhelmed.
- Feeling that something hurts – you seem to have a growing list of aches and pains.
- Muscle tension.
- Not having enough physical activity and exercise.
- Feeling irritable; little things easily annoy you.
- Poor sleep quality.
- Recurring chronic or serious illness (colds, flu-like symptoms, infections).
- Lack of peace and quiet.
- Feeling down after too long on social media.
- Lack of regular meals.
- Eating a lot of crap.
- Anxiety and worry.
- Your mind won't shut off.
- Low-level depression.
- Feeling trapped by obligations and commitments.
- Not enough time for family or friends.
- Working too much.
- An inability to say no to others' needs and demands.

- Feelings of emptiness, disconnection, and loneliness.
- Negative and self-sabotaging thoughts.
- Low self-esteem and confidence.

In 2017, in an article for (now defunct) *The Pool* www .the-pool.com, author Marie Phillips described experiencing 'a mini burnout':

'I was miserable all the time, lacking in energy, unwilling to see friends and unable to work. I tried and tried to feel happier, forcing myself to soldier on and put on a smiling face. Nothing worked ... I decided that I wasn't going to try to feel happy any more. I decided that I needed to look after myself better, not in order to be happy, but to stop myself from getting so overwhelmed in the future.'

Marie decided to take better care of her physical and mental health. Amongst other things, she said:

'I've improved my diet (less meat, more veg); I limit myself to no more than two alcoholic drinks per night (this is the thing I've done that has had the single largest impact on my anxiety); I take more exercise (walking or cycling every day, plus I've taken up rowing); I meditate daily ... I found a life coach who taught me, among other things, to have better boundaries; I stopped reading the news because it was killing me with stress; I turn down work I really don't want to do even if it's well paid ... and I've rearranged my living arrangements with my boyfriend so that I can work from home.'

Marie wrote: 'The key thing, though, is that none of it is aimed at turning me into a happy person' but after six months of healthy living, she realized that she did feel much happier.

'By focusing on being healthy, I've crept up on happiness from the side – I feel calm and rested; I'm enjoying work again; I'm more present as a partner and a friend. Perhaps all along I already had what I needed in my life to feel happy, but only in working on my health did I become well enough to appreciate it.'

Self-Care; Self-Indulgent?

Self-care, like mindfulness, might appear to be the latest new 'thing' and yet, like mindfulness, it's not a recent phenomenon; it's not a new concept. Over two thousand years ago the Greek philosopher Socrates spoke of the need to prioritize self-care. *Epimeleia heautou* – care of the self – is central to Socratic ethics: the moral principles of what makes for 'right conduct.'

Socrates' emphasis on the importance of paying attention to oneself in order to be as good as possible may seem self-indulgent and selfish, but there is an inseparable link between self-care and care for others in Socratic ethics. Far from being at the expense of others, self-care is bound to the care of others.

As my wise friend Alex says: 'there is so much we can do to help the world, our communities, our friends and families but this all starts with me. I am of no use to anyone until I can take care of myself ... when we transform ourselves, first we are doing service for the world ... the most important thing is to balance our physical, emotional and mental lives so we function as integrated personalities and are actually of use to others.'

And, when it comes to our health, the Self Care Forum point out that 'in many cases people can take care of their minor ailments, reducing the number of GP consultations and enabling GPs to focus on caring for higher risk patients, such as those with comorbidities (the presence of additional conditions co-occurring with a primary condition), the very young and elderly, managing long-term conditions and providing new services.

More cost-effective use of stretched NHS resources allows money to be spent where it's most needed and improve health outcomes. Furthermore, increased personal responsibility around healthcare helps improve people's health and wellbeing and better manage long-term conditions when they do develop. This will ultimately ensure the long-term sustainability of the NHS.'

Self-care is not selfish, self-centred, or self-indulgent. It's self-respectful. It's also respectful and considerate of others.

When you fly on an airplane, the flight attendant instructs: 'If there should be a change in cabin pressure, put your oxygen mask on first before helping others.' Because if you run out of oxygen, you can't help anyone else with their oxygen mask. This analogy is often used to describe the importance of self-care. It's a good analogy, but it's flawed. Why? Because running out of oxygen is an emergency. If you waited for emergencies before implementing self-care you'd be at crisis point: managing burnout, exhaustion, and health problems.

What's Stopping You?

But if your life is busy, finding the time and energy and remembering to take proper care of yourself can fall by the wayside. If you're feeling down, distracted, worried, or anxious self-care can seem like far too big an effort. And if you're stressed, unwell, or exhausted, experiencing bereavement, trauma, or a major challenge and perhaps most in most need of it, self-care can feel like an especially tall order, even when you know it will help you to feel better.

But being busy, feeling tired, being down, or feeling overwhelmed are the signs that you really need self-care; self-care that's calming and comforting, healing and restorative.

Self-discipline is self-caring.

M. Scott Peck

Perhaps, though, the idea of self-care sounds limiting; dull and boring. Not so! Not every choice has to be 'self-care'. There's always a time for a late night instead of an early night, a time for one more drink, a time for pizza and chocolate cake for breakfast, for not leaving the sofa all weekend. In fact, if you're already taking good care of yourself, you can easily indulge in some guilty pleasures, with no need to feel guilty at all!

Self-Care Actions

Take responsibility for yourself. Don't use whatever's going on in your life as an excuse for a lack of self care. Don't blame other people; their needs and demands, either. Take responsibility for your mental, emotional, physical health and well-being.

Know that self-care is not selfish. It's not self-centred or self-indulgent. Self-care is self-respectful. It's also respectful and considerate of others.

PART I

Care for Your Mind

2
Accept Yourself

*No amount of self-improvement can make up for any
lack of self-acceptance.*

Robert Holden

Self-care starts with the acknowledgement that you're
worth taking care of. Self-acceptance is related to
self-esteem. But where self-esteem is concerned with
how well you regard yourself, self-acceptance acknowledges and accepts the less positive, less 'esteem-able'
parts; self-acceptance acknowledges and accepts your
failings and foibles and doesn't let your shortcomings
define you or undermine your true worth.

Can you accept and approve of yourself despite any failings or foibles, limitations or weaknesses? Yes. You can.

But why might you, like so many of us, think negatively
about yourself and your abilities? There are a number
of reasons. Being put down, criticized, humiliated,

bullied, discriminated, or left out by others can leave you with low levels of self-worth. If you are under pressure, stressed and finding it hard to cope, or you have overly high standards and unrealistic expectations for yourself – about who you 'should' be and what you 'should' be able to do – this too can lead to negative thinking about yourself when you don't meet those high expectations.

How often, for example, do you give yourself a hard time when you make a mistake, or you screw up? Do you feel really bad if you think you've upset someone else or let someone down? Perhaps you still feel guilty for something you said or did to someone else. Do you blame yourself if things don't turn out the way you hoped? Or maybe you berate yourself when you're unable to cope with a particular situation. When you look at social media – Twitter, Instagram and Facebook – do you ever think that everyone else is living a lovely life; you compare your situation with theirs and find yours wanting? You doubt yourself, your abilities, and your achievements and tell yourself things like 'I'm not good enough. I'll never match up.'

We all have an inner voice; what's known as 'self-talk'. It provides us with a running commentary rather like the constant text at the bottom of 24-hour news channels. It is this inner voice that directs your thinking and shapes your beliefs and actions. Mostly, your self-talk is neutral; observations and acknowledgements of day-to-day events such as: 'It's raining, I'll need an umbrella' or 'I must remember to buy some milk'.

Your self-talk can also be positive, encouraging, and empowering when you think, for example, about a particular situation: 'I can give it a try. I'm pleased with how I did that. Well done me!' But your self-talk can also criticize and judge you, belittle and berate you. You might say things to yourself such as: 'I'm never going to be able to work this out', 'Why does this happen to me?, 'People will think I'm stupid', 'I look like shit', or 'I always say the wrong thing'.

But everything you say to yourself matters! Negative self-talk from your inner critic – that disapproving voice inside your head – can leave you feeling inadequate and hopeless. It inhibits you, limits you, erodes your peace of mind and emotional wellbeing. It doesn't allow room for self-acceptance.

Catch the Critic

Self-acceptance is my refusal to be in an adversarial relationship with myself.

Nathaniel Branden

Your thoughts are so powerful *because* you rarely have conscious awareness or control over them. More often than not, you won't even notice when you're thinking in negative ways; berating and reprimanding yourself and bringing yourself down. So, to gain control over your inner critic you have to first be aware of it; to make a conscious effort to slow down and pay more attention to your thoughts and self-talk.

To begin with, your emotions can alert you to the presence of your inner critic. Whenever you're feeling worried, disappointed, stressed, angry or upset, guilty or regretful about something you have or haven't done, stop and be aware of your thoughts.

A good exercise to try for one week is to keep an 'inner critic log', either in a notebook or on your phone. If you notice yourself being self-critical, just note a few words about the situation – *Overslept again. Snapped at the kids/partner/parent/colleague. Ate too much. Drank too much. Didn't get everything done* – and what the criticism was – *I'm crap at getting up on time. Why can't I be nice? They probably hate me! I have no self-control! What's wrong with me?* Once you're aware of the critical voice, you're in a better position to disempower it.

Challenge Your Inner Critic

> *Tell the negative committee that meets inside your head to sit down and shut up.*
>
> Ann Bradford

So often, the negative self-talk that comes from your inner critic goes unchallenged. Self-talk goes on in your head; unless you say it out loud, other people aren't aware of what you're saying to yourself and so can't tell you that you're being too hard on yourself, that you're being unreasonable, illogical, or that your inner voice is just plain wrong. So, your mind simply accepts everything you tell it and you respond accordingly.

What, then, to do? There are a number of things you can try.

Give the Inner Critic a Name

There's someone in my head but it's not me.

Roger Waters

One thing you can try is to separate the critical voice from yourself. You can do this by giving it a name – Ursula, Skeletor – any political, celebrity, or fictional character whose name resonates as an unkind person for you. When you name the critical voice as belonging to someone else it loses some of its power.

By separating the inner critic from yourself, it's no longer you saying it, it's them. We don't tend to become defensive against ourselves, but we are more likely to get defensive against external comments; what someone else says. Separating the inner critic from yourself can help you realize how unkind and unhelpful the comments are and that you don't have to agree with them. So, try giving the negative voice in your head a name and any time you're aware of thinking something negative about yourself, tell that name to stop it; that they're being negative, unhelpful, and unfair.

Stop That Thought

Simply telling your inner critic you aren't going to listen to what it has to say begins to give you a sense of choice in the matter. When you hear that inner critic start to speak and say, for example, 'I've made an idiot of myself', 'I'll never be able to do this', 'I shouldn't have done that', or 'I'm being selfish', refuse to listen. Tell it you refuse to listen.

Have a phrase or word that stops the train of negative self-talk. If you find yourself slipping back into 'I'm crap. I'm hopeless' simply say 'Stop!' to yourself. Images can help; you might want to visualize a red stop sign. Or tell yourself 'No, I'm not going there. I'm not thinking like that!' Then refocus your thoughts to more positive, helpful, kind thoughts and self-talk.

You might want to try using a thought-changing prompt. When you notice that negative thoughts or images are starting to enter your mind, in order to prompt you not to listen and, instead, to come up with alternative more positive, helpful thoughts, try one of these:

- If you're sitting down, stand up.
- If you're standing up, sit down.
- If you're indoors go to a different room.
- If you're out walking, cross to the other side of the road. Or, you can change the direction you're walking; take 20 steps in the opposite direction before turning around and going back the way you were going.

Engage with Your Inner Advocate

But how do you replace unhelpful and disempowering thoughts and beliefs about yourself with more realistic, useful, and empowering ones? By having an even stronger ally on your side. You need to engage with your inner advocate. Where the inner critic is that voice in your head that's quick to judge and is ready with a put-down, your inner advocate is the other voice in your head – the positive voice – the one that defends and encourages you.

When your inner critic puts you down, your inner advocate steps in and presents a kinder, more gentle perspective on your behalf. While your inner critic is against you, your inner advocate is for you, it supports you. Your inner advocate is kind. So, next time you realize you're berating yourself, make the deliberate effort to say something different to yourself and find evidence to support the more positive thought. When you hear your inner critic saying, for example, 'I'm hopeless at ...', put your hand on your heart and speak supportively and with kindness to yourself, as a good friend would do. Tell the critic 'You're being harsh. You're *not* hopeless. You're just not as good at ... as you'd like to be. But you *can* get better. You've learnt to ... so you know you can learn to do this, too. It just takes time.'

Recognize that Critical Thoughts Aren't Helping You

Challenging negative thoughts and looking for alternative, fairer, more positive thoughts can be an effective way to manage negative self-talk. Something else you can do whenever you catch yourself thinking negative thoughts about yourself, is to ask yourself 'In what way are these thoughts helping me?'

Perhaps you can remember a recent difficult, stressful event or situation for which you blamed or berated yourself. Maybe you lost or broke something, you didn't manage to achieve something, or you let someone down. What were your thoughts likely to have been? Did your self-talk make the situation easier in any way? Did your self-talk help you feel better about yourself?

When you ask yourself 'Are these thoughts helpful?' you're not disputing the accuracy of your thoughts; you're not arguing with yourself as to whether or not you're hopeless or no good at something. Regardless of their accuracy, these thoughts are not helping you; getting stuck in negative self-talk is not making you feel good. So, in future, when you catch yourself thinking negatively, remind yourself that negative self-talk doesn't help you feel good about yourself and your abilities. Ask yourself 'In what way is it helpful for me to think like this?'

What if the critic is true, though? It doesn't matter. Negative self-talk is never in your interest. Even if you have screwed up or made a fool of yourself in some way, there's always a different, kinder, better way to treat yourself that doesn't involve negative labels and destructive criticism. In any given situation you can focus on what you did wrong or you can accept what you did wrong and what you can do better next time.

If, for example, after a period of time you're still reproaching yourself for having failed an exam, or an interview, ask yourself, in what way is thinking like this helpful? Wallowing in 'I'm crap. No one is going to want to employ me' isn't helpful. It's self-pity. Sure, for whatever reason, you failed. Acknowledge that. You can then choose whether to dwell on it or move on to more positive, encouraging and helpful thoughts; thoughts about what you can do to improve and what you can do to make a situation better.

Moving on to Positive Thoughts

There's a mindful concept known as 'acceptance and commitment' that can help you let go of unhelpful thoughts and move on to helpful thoughts. An acceptance and commitment approach suggests that you don't challenge or argue with the inner critic. You don't tell it it's being unfair and unkind. Instead, you simply notice and accept that you're thinking negatively about yourself. Then you let those thoughts go and move on to more helpful ways of thinking, responding, and behaving.

Supposing, for example, your thoughts about something were: 'I've made a right mess of this. I'm hopeless.' Whether your thinking is correct or not, you simply acknowledge and *accept* that it's not helping you to continue thinking in this way and you move on to thinking – to *committing* yourself to – more helpful thoughts and solutions. So, in this example, you'd accept that maybe you did or maybe you didn't make a mess of something and maybe you are or maybe you aren't hopeless. Whatever. The important thing would be to *accept* that what's done is in the past and think about how you could move on from there – what you could *commit* to doing now, in the present, to move forward in a positive way.

Acceptance and commitment recognizes that when you accept and let go of negative unhelpful thoughts, you let go of the emotional aspects and allow the rational, logical part of your mind to start working for you; to think in more helpful, positive ways.

Be mindful; know that all the time you are berating yourself for something that happened days, weeks, months, or even years ago you are living in the past; you're letting the hurt and pain burden you by holding onto it. And that's not being kind to yourself or caring. Whatever you did or didn't do, think about what you would say to someone else in the same situation to make them feel better. What kind, helpful things would you say to a friend? How would you reassure them? What would you suggest they do?

Now, do that for yourself.

The Power of 'But' and 'And'

A useful way to change negative, unhelpful thoughts into more helpful thoughts is to follow the negative thought with a 'but' and then complete the sentence. So, whenever you catch yourself saying something negative about yourself, add the word 'but'. This prompts you to follow up with a positive sentence.

- I've let my friend down because I forgot about our night out together, *but* I could ...
- I didn't do well in the interview, but ...

Get Some Perspective

Tout comprendre, c'est tout pardonner (To understand all is to pardon all).

It helps if you can gain a bit of perspective. Gaining perspective means getting a sense of where what you did or didn't do fits into the greater scheme of things. It's taking a step back from yourself and seeing yourself through different eyes; from someone else's kindly perspective; responding to yourself with the same understanding as a friend would offer for what you did or didn't do.

Perspective helps you to understand that whenever you feel bad about what you did or didn't do, you need to put it in context; take into account all the circumstances or facts that surround a particular situation that you're giving yourself a hard time about.

Supposing, for example, you regret something you did or said. Perhaps you regret telling someone what you really thought of them, maybe you regret that you took this job, or had another drink or piece of cake. Conversely, you might regret something you *didn't* do or say; you didn't say sorry, you didn't work hard enough or try hard enough, you failed to stand up for yourself or support someone else, you didn't take that job, or you regret not finishing a relationship sooner.

Consider the circumstances at the time you did or didn't do something. Maybe you had no way of knowing what the consequences would be; perhaps you were under pressure and stressed or had other commitments or limited support. Maybe you had an unmet need. Did you misunderstand or not know all the facts about a situation? Be kind to yourself; know that, whatever it was, you did it based on what you knew or were able to do at the time.

And if it was something you didn't do, know now that not doing something was also based on the cir-cumstances and conditions at the time. Perhaps, for example, you failed to speak up for or support someone else. Maybe at the time, you were involved with your own concerns, or you didn't realize they needed your support, or you didn't want to get too involved.

Know that taking the relevant circumstances into account doesn't make your action or inaction right or wrong. It doesn't let you off the hook. It just explains why you did or didn't do something. You had good reasons at the time. Now you know or feel differently. What we can handle and how we handle it varies from one time to another. It's easy in hindsight to see the realities, possibilities, or requirements of a situation or decision after it happened.

Tell yourself the whole story. Not just one aspect. See *everything* that has happened as a result of what you did or didn't do. Not just the negative aspects, but also what lessons you learned from it.

See that what's happened is part of the grander scheme of things. One way to do this is to think about how you will view your mistake, what you did wrong, or failed to achieve a month from now. How about a year from now? Two years, five years? Acknowledge that you're continuing to grow into the person you're becoming, and that the person you are right now also deserves kindness.

Self-acceptance happens in the present, it's not future oriented, as in: 'I'll feel good about myself when …' or 'As soon as I achieve or succeed with … I'll be OK'. With self-acceptance you can absolutely accept where you are at any given moment, while also holding space for being more; for being, for example, more patient, more careful, or more understanding. For being a better parent, friend, or whatever it is you would like to be.

Accepting where you're at and that you're OK doesn't mean you can't move forward. It means that you recognize there are times when, just like everyone else, you won't be, for example, tactful or polite or grateful, that there are times when you'll say something hurtful, be rude or thoughtless.

Give yourself a break where you fall short and accept that, in many things, you're a bit crap. Recognize that more often than not, good enough is good enough. Even no good at all – because we're all no good at many things – can be OK. Really. Take a reality check; knowing you simply can't do and be anything and everything is the only realistic response to the things you can't change, the talents and looks you weren't born with, the skills you're unlikely to acquire.

Think of things you don't like. Perhaps you don't like brussels sprouts or mustard. Do you berate yourself for it? If you don't like brussels sprouts or mustard and can accept it, then you can accept that, for example, you're not very tidy or that you can't concentrate on any one thing for long periods of time.

I accept that I'm never going to visit Thailand or Vietnam. I'm just not that interested. I like reality TV shows such as 'I'm a Celebrity' and 'First Dates'. But I don't like 'Love Island' even though many people I know think it's brilliant. I don't understand cricket and I think golf is boring. I'm hopeless at playing any sport. I'm impatient, and sometimes that's a good thing – it means I get things done and I move on quite quickly from difficulties. I would have liked to have been a backing singer in a rock 'n' roll band. I never was or will be. I can (just about) accept that.

Like me, your likes and dislikes, failings and foibles are all just part of who you are. Stop trying to be perfect. Stop with the 'I'm not enough; I'm not good enough/

clever enough/decisive enough/nice enough' type of self-talk and replace it with 'I am enough. Tomorrow I can strive to be more, but right now, I'm enough.'

Rather than berate yourself, accept yourself. Berating yourself is self-harm. Accepting yourself is self-care.

Be Aware of the Comparison Trap

If you judge a fish by its ability to climb a tree, it will live its whole life believing that it is stupid.
Albert Einstein

Too often, we compare ourselves with someone who we think is 'better' or has more. The problem is, there's always someone you know, meet, see, listen to, or read about in the news, or on social media, who you could see as being 'better': more successful, better looking, more capable, or who has more and has done better or done more than you.

You can always find ways that you don't match up; there's always a gap between yourself and someone else. Of course, it's natural to want to know where you fit into the scheme of things. But measuring your worth and your abilities against other people and concluding you don't match up can only lead to feeling inferior; feeling disappointed and maybe even ashamed.

Comparing yourself with someone else – who they are and what they have – means you can only see what

they've got and what you haven't. But negative compar-
isons can undermine your confidence and self-esteem
and leave you feeling inadequate. Why would you want
to make yourself miserable? You wouldn't do that to a
friend; you wouldn't be unkind enough to point out to
your friend in what ways they don't match up and are
less than others.

Too often, we compare ourselves with someone who we
think is 'better' or has more: better skills, abilities, or
personal qualities and better or more resources and pos-
sessions. We compare what we think is the worst of ourselves to the best we presume about others. But other
people have crap times; they have bad days too, who-
ever they are, whatever their abilities. On 3 May 2019
Scottish distance runner Eilish McColgan made a post
on social media describing her day from hell:

> So I was tempted to just pretend last night didn't happen
> and continue on that running is all rainbows and unicorns,
> but then I thought 'why do athletes avoid their bad days?'
>
> Everyone loves to boast about the good days – but some-
> times we just have shit days.
>
> 5 days before the race, I picked up a shin injury from abso-
> lutely nowhere. Training had been good and then about an
> hour after I received a text from a UKA physio asking how
> things were – I got a sharp pain in my shin. (That's voodoo
> doll sort of stuff.)
>
> I was advised not to race but after 5 days of icing my leg
> like a lunatic – it started to ease a little. And Michael acted
> like some sort of magician with a teaspoon, massaging it
> the night before which reduced the pain too.

I warmed up with my leg essentially gaffer-taped together by K tape & Walmart compression socks and felt it was manageable to race.

During my warm up, I then took my period. Whichever God created ovaries is an arse hole. 99% of the time when I take my period on race day or a few days before racing/ training – I run like dog shit. Feeling heavy, flat and like a walrus trying to run around in circles. I took a heap of painkillers to stop my stomach from feeling like a horse was kicking me in the ovaries and set off in the race hoping for a minor miracle to get me round 25 laps.

In all honesty, the shin held up pretty well, I commited (sic) to the race and followed the pacer, but my legs were getting heavier and heavier after just a mile. I think I made it to 5 laps to go before calling it a day.

I called my mum, cried a little, walked to McDonald's where they refused to serve us at the drive thru because we didn't have a car, proceeded to walk to Safeway and bought a $8.99 Red Velvet cake for my tea before sitting up to 5am feeling sorry for myself and over thinking every day of my life for the last 28 years.

I then woke up this morning, posted a picture on Instagram and proceeded to move the f*** on! So there you have it – an honest account of a professional athletes life when they have a bit of a shit day! This doesn't even rank in the top 5 shitty days of 2019 so far … so let's take that as a positive.

Eilish's Instagram followers felt both relieved and encouraged. 'Massively helpful to average runners like me. Bravo Eilish', wrote one.

'Thanks for sharing your human side. It's easy to think elite athletes train all day every day, don't eat cake and do run like lightning. It's good to be reminded that our sporting heroes have similar challenges to the rest of us', said another follower.

'What a breath of fresh air to read this. Insta only shows the highs so we think people are perfect. Well done for being so honest', said another.

And someone else wrote: 'This is going to help so many young female athletes who read your post.'

Too often, we don't recognize one of the most basic truths about being human: that we fail. Too often, we believe the opposite; that we can and *should* do well in everything. Even when faced with something overwhelming such as a serious illness, injury, or trauma we feel the pressure to cope and to manage. When I was writing this book, a friend of mine was diagnosed with terminal cancer. She told me that several friends and family members were urging her to be brave and strong; that she *must* fight the cancer and get better. Their remarks, although well intentioned, upset and annoyed her. She explained 'There's nothing I can do but accept the cancer; not fight it and feel that on top of everything else, I'm failing; failing to stay alive.'

Kindness and compassion for yourself both stem from the same thing: understanding the human condition. That is, understanding what it means to be human. We get ill and we get diseases. We love and we hate. We have flaws and weaknesses, failings, foibles, and imperfections. There are always going to be things we can't do, things we can't be; there are always going to be mistakes that we make.

Self-acceptance doesn't depend on being perfect; on never doing anything wrong. Self-acceptance means understanding that you're human, that it's human to have flaws and failings, but that they don't completely define you. You still have value and worth.

You may not have come up to scratch in some way, but you're still a good person. See yourself as a person of worth; doing the best you can with what you have.

Self-Care Actions

Be more aware of your inner critic. Whenever you're feeling worried, disappointed, stressed, angry, upset, guilty about something you have or haven't done, stop and be aware of your thoughts. You might want to try keeping an 'inner critic log'. If you notice yourself being self-critical, just note a few words about the situation and what the criticism was.

Try giving the inner critic a name. Then, any time you're aware of thinking something negative about yourself, tell that name to stop it; that they're being mean and unfair.

Stop self-critical thoughts. Refuse to listen. Simply say 'Stop!' to yourself. Or 'No, I'm not going there. I'm not thinking like that!' Or try using a thought-changing prompt; if you're sitting down, stand up. If you're standing up, sit down. If you're indoors go to a different room. If you're out walking, cross to the other side of the road or change the direction you're walking.

Recognize that critical thoughts aren't helpful. Ask yourself: 'In what way are these thoughts helping me?' Whenever you catch yourself saying something negative about yourself, add the word 'but'. This prompts you to follow up with a positive sentence.

Engage with your inner advocate. Instead of berating yourself, say something positive about yourself and find evidence to support the more positive thought.

Try an acceptance and commitment approach. Notice and accept that you're thinking negatively about yourself. Then let those thoughts go and commit to more positive, helpful thoughts.

Get things into perspective. Don't just see the negative aspects, think too, what lessons you've learnt from what did or didn't happen. Think about how you will view a mistake, a failure, or a wrongdoing a month from now. Will it be such a big deal? How about a year from now? Two years, five years?

Be aware of comparing yourself with someone else. Comparing yourself with who they are and what they have means you can only see what they've got and what you haven't.

See yourself as a person of worth; doing the best you can with what you have. Rather than berate yourself, accept yourself. Berating yourself is self-harm. Accepting yourself is self-care.

3
Feel Good About Yourself

We ask ourselves, Who am I to be brilliant, gorgeous, talented, and fabulous? Actually, who are you not to be? ... We are all meant to shine, as children do ... It is not just in some of us; it is in everyone.

Marianne Williamson

When you cease judging and berating yourself and being so hard on yourself; when you can accept yourself more, then self-esteem – recognizing your worth and liking yourself – rises naturally. But even when you *are* more able to accept yourself, low self-esteem can still sneak up on you and bring you down.

So what can help to develop and raise your self-esteem? There are a number of things. To begin with, you need an inner voice that acts as your own best friend; a positive inner voice that regularly notices and acknowledges the good things about yourself; your strengths; the things that you shine at.

Let's start with your personal qualities; your distinctive characteristics and attributes. Read through this list and as you do, tick *each and every* quality that applies to you:

- Adaptable
- Altruistic
- Caring
- Cooperative
- Courteous
- Dependable
- Diplomatic
- Empathic
- Encouraging
- Fair
- Flexible
- Friendly
- Hardworking
- Helpful
- Innovative
- Loyal
- Meticulous
- Observant
- Open-minded
- Optimistic
- Organized
- Perceptive
- Persistent
- Reassuring
- Reliable
- Resourceful
- Responsible

- Sense of humour
- Sincere
- Sociable
- Sympathetic
- Thorough
- Tolerant
- Trustworthy
- Truthful
- Understanding.

Now, from all those that you've ticked, choose your top five qualities: the five qualities that you think best describe you.

Next, for each quality, think about how and why you have this quality. Think of a time or times when you've used that quality. Write down your thoughts and ideas. So, for example, if you felt that being open-minded was one of your qualities, you might write: 'I can listen to someone else's opinions and ideas, without immediately making assumptions or jumping to conclusions.' Your example might be: 'When a colleague suggested we do something in a different way, unlike others who derided her idea, I asked questions and asked for more information before I decided if her idea could work.'

If another one of your qualities was persistence, you might say: 'I can keep going with a task, especially in the face of difficulties. I overcome setbacks, find new ways to move forward and carry on. I did this recently when I was pursuing the health care I felt I needed.'

If another one of your qualities was that you were tactful, you might say: 'In sensitive situations I know how to be honest while, at the same time, avoid giving offence. I did this when I …'

And if being reliable was one of your qualities, you might have written: 'I can be trusted and depended on to do what I say I will. Friends have told me how much they value this about me.'

Ask yourself questions to help you to think and write about your good qualities:

- How might I have helped someone with this quality?
- What challenges have I overcome by having this quality?
- How has this quality helped me in my work or day-to-day life?

When you have low feelings of self-worth, your negative thoughts distort your perception of yourself and you overlook the positives. Identifying your good qualities and explaining how, why, and when you have each quality can help you to see your own worth and so help boost your self-esteem.

Acknowledge your positive qualities and things you are good at. Get into the habit of identifying and thinking positive things about yourself. Write down these personal affirmations – these truths about yourself – and keep them where you can read them as and when you need to. And if you have difficulty with identifying and coming up with examples of your qualities, ask someone who knows you and who you trust to help you. They'll come up with things you might not see in yourself.

Recognize Your Skills

As well as identifying and acknowledging your qualities, identify and acknowledge other personal attributes that you have: your skills. Your skills are the things that you do well as a result of an innate talent or the things you do well as a result of learning and/or practising and becoming experienced in doing.

Identify skills you've acquired through work, study, hobbies, and interests. Think of the skills you've learnt that are a part of your job. Perhaps you work in sales, retail, or admin? Maybe you work in the medical profession, education, finance, IT, hospitality, or animal welfare? Maybe your job is an administrative one or you work in construction? What skills have you developed? Write them down.

Do you have any hobbies or interests? What skills have you acquired as a result of those hobbies or interests? Maybe you're a good cook or gardener? You might play a musical instrument? Perhaps you're good at fixing and mending things?

Ask yourself some questions about your skills. Ask yourself: 'How has this skill enhanced my life? Have I helped someone by having this skill?'

Write down your skills. Add to your list whenever you think of something – a personal quality and strength, a skill, an ability – at which you shine. Add something about your physical appearance that you like as well. Ask other people what they think you're good at and add those strengths and talents to your list. Good things other people say about you may be about your skills, but could also be about a good deed you did, for example.

Recognize Your Efforts, Achievements, and Successes

Think of the last time you achieved something. Maybe you finished a difficult project or learnt something new? Perhaps you passed a test or exam? Did you do something that required some courage on your part – perhaps you stood up to someone or walked away from a bad situation of some sort? Maybe you finally got around to completing some small task you'd been putting off for ages – decorating a room, sorting out a pile of paperwork, or cleaning out the fridge?

Of course, achievements come in all shapes and sizes but whatever it was, did you take the time to acknowledge your achievement or did you simply move on to the next thing without stopping to reflect, to acknowledge, and to congratulate yourself?

Acknowledging your achievements, even in a small way, increases your self-esteem. So be more aware of your achievements and give yourself some recognition;

when you do something you're pleased about, stop for a minute and recognize it. Compliment yourself; tell yourself 'Good for me! I've done OK' or 'That went well, I'm pleased with myself' or 'That was bloody hard. But I did it' or 'All that effort paid off. Well done me!' or 'Hurrah! I'm brilliant!'

Identify and write down situations where you have done well and felt good about yourself in the past. When you feel your self-esteem is slipping, remind yourself of these times as a way of helping you to have positive thoughts and images of yourself.

Take a Compliment

As well as recognizing your positive qualities, skills, abilities, and achievements, do you accept the recognition that other people give you? If someone gives you a compliment, do you accept it and allow it to make you feel good? Or do you brush it off? Perhaps you don't want to appear immodest or the compliment or praise doesn't line up with how you see yourself. But when someone gives you a compliment it's the same as if they were giving you a gift. Therefore if you reject the compliment it's like rejecting and refusing to accept a gift. And that's not nice, is it? It's not nice and it's not being kind to yourself or to the other person.

Next time someone says something positive about you, decide to accept what they're saying as a real possibility; that it *is* possible that, for example, you look great; that your hair looks nice today or that what you're wearing really suits you. Or that you've been thoughtful and considerate, and it's made a positive difference to someone. Or that you do something really well.

Believe the other person; they're being nice and they're being genuine, aren't they? Be gracious; accept a compliment in the same way you would accept a gift; just say 'Thank you'. And if you say more than that, simply say 'How nice, thank you.' Or, 'Thank you. I really appreciate you telling me.'

Do Things You Enjoy

> *And now that you don't have to be perfect, you can be good.*
>
> John Steinbeck

As well as recognizing and acknowledging the ways you shine, self-esteem can also be increased by doing things that you enjoy. We're all usually quite good at the things we enjoy, and we usually enjoy doing the things we're good at. What do you like doing? Swimming, painting, or yoga? Maybe you enjoy singing? Fishing? Playing a musical instrument? Running? Playing football? Taking part in historical re-enactments?

The more often you do things you like doing and can do well, the more often you feel good *because* you're doing something you enjoy and can do well; you have positive thoughts about the activity and about yourself doing it. It could be something creative: painting, cooking, sewing, or writing, for example. It might be a physical activity: gardening or hiking, for example; horse riding or tennis. It might be something you do on your own – reading, painting, gardening – or with other people – team sports, board and computer games, singing in a choir, hiking.

Whatever it is that you like doing – do it more often! Find what you enjoy doing and do more of it. You don't have to excel at an activity, you just need to like it and be good enough at it. If, for example, you enjoy cooking and you're a good cook, invite people round for a meal more often. If you're a good runner, sign up for races.

Self-Care Actions

Know that being preoccupied with what's 'wrong' and trying to fix it is an uphill struggle. A more positive, self-caring approach builds on what you are doing right.

Acknowledge your positive qualities and things you are good at. Get into the habit of identifying and thinking positive things about yourself. Write down these personal affirmations – these truths about yourself – and keep them where you can read them as and when you need to.

Listen to others. If you have difficulty with identifying and coming up with examples of your qualities, ask someone who knows you and who you trust. They'll come up with things you might not see in yourself. Write down good things that other people say about you, too.

Be more aware of your achievements and give yourself some recognition. When you do something you're pleased about, stop for a minute and recognize it. Compliment yourself; tell yourself 'Good for me! I've done OK.'

Accept a compliment. Next time someone says something positive about you, decide to accept what they're saying as a real possibility. Believe the other person; they're being nice and they're being genuine. Make a note of them to look over when you feel your self-esteem is slipping; when you're feeling low or doubting yourself.

Enjoy yourself more often! Find what you enjoy doing and do more of it. You don't have to excel at an activity, you just need to like it and be good enough at it. The more often you do things you like doing and can do well, the more often you feel good *because* you're doing something you enjoy and can do well; you have positive thoughts about the activity and about yourself doing it.

4

Stop Doing so Much

Slow down and enjoy life. It's not only the scenery you miss by going too fast; you also miss the sense of where you're going and why.

Eddie Cantor

What's a typical week for you? What do you have to do next? What haven't you done? Is there too much to do and too much to think about? Are you trying to cope with what you haven't done and what you've yet to do and you're doing several things at once? It's difficult to think clearly; you feel anxious, frustrated, overwhelmed, and stressed. And life is just racing by. While you like the idea of taking time for yourself – to take better care of yourself – there just aren't enough hours in the day. You've got too much to do and too little time to do it in. And very little time for self-care.

If all this sounds like you then, most likely, you're not saying 'no' enough.

Too often, we commit to too many people and too many things, and then find ourselves without enough time to do anything properly and no time to switch off. Maybe you're in a book club and you've taken out a gym membership or you've taken on some voluntary work. Perhaps you've joined a committee, enrolled on a course, and got involved in a local, national, or even a global cause. You might have agreed to attend a friend's play, art show, band or choir performance, or cheer a colleague on as they run a marathon. And you've got a birthday party to organize, homework to help with, a camping trip coming up, a DIY project to finish, and the gardening to do.

And that's just your home, family, and social life! How did it get to this?

Maybe you're the sort of person who over-commits when you're feeling particularly positive and optimistic about what you're able to do. At the time when you decide to take something on, you think you'll be able to manage. So you agree to another chore or errand, task or project and the duties, responsibilities, and obligations that come with it.

Maybe you sign up to causes and offer to help others out of goodwill and compassion or you feel strongly about an issue and you really want to step up for the cause. Or perhaps you simply can't say no to invites; to Friday evening drinks with colleagues, for example, or to be part of a sports team. It could be that you find it difficult to turn down other people's requests for help: to look after their dog and feed their cat when they go on holiday or to help them with some DIY.

We can get so used to saying yes to commitments and other people that we lose sight of what we do and don't want and what our own needs are. But if your life is so tightly packed that you don't have time for what really matters – your physical and mental health – it's time to make a change and apply some self-care.

Why Can't You Let Go?

Of course, taking a step back and disengaging from some commitments isn't always easy. It may be that you're thinking about sunk costs; the time, effort, love, or money you've already put into something. Even though you now regret having got involved, it would be a waste of what you've already put into it. You've done it for so long already, you tell yourself that you might as well carry on.

Perhaps you worry that if you drop out, you'll be letting people down. You said you'd do something, and now you feel it's your duty – you should keep your word, stick with it, and put up with the inconvenience. You think they can't do it without you, that they *need* you and you can't let them down. You feel trapped, but you're concerned that if you pull out the other person or people won't be able to cope. Perhaps you can't face their reaction; you worry that they will be upset or angry with you.

It could be that a particular commitment is no longer relevant or appropriate in your life, but you don't know how to tell others that you no longer want to be involved. And maybe you don't want to call it a day because you don't want to admit that you were wrong to have committed to it in the first place. So instead of letting go, you struggle on.

That's not self-care! Self-care isn't something that obligates you, depletes, and drains you. Self-care is something that allows you time and space.

If you're feeling overwhelmed and overburdened, then letting go of some of your commitments will give you more time, energy, and headspace to better look after yourself. Not only will you feel less pressured and less stressed *doing* less, but you'll feel less stressed just not having to *think* about what you 'ought' to be doing or what you 'should' be doing.

Identify Your Commitments

If you're overwhelmed with how much you have going on with your home, family and social life, something has to give. You need to set yourself some limits. Self-care – effectively caring for yourself – involves knowing what is and isn't important for you – what you do and don't need – and acting on it. Are there things you can drop so that you have more time for you?

Start by thinking of everything (apart from work; we'll look at that later) you've got going on in a typical day, week, and month:

- Tasks and chores at home – cooking cleaning, mending, fixing, decorating.
- Family members' needs and activities to attend to.
- Your own hobbies, interests, projects, clubs, voluntary work.
- Friends and social life.

No matter how big or small the activity, task, chore, responsibility etc. write them down. Write down daily, weekly, and monthly tasks, chores, activities, and commitments.

Now, which of the things on your list do you recognize as things you absolutely *have* to do – cook, clean, care for someone else: for example, children or a vulnerable family member? These are the activities, tasks, and duties that are probably non-negotiable – you need or have to keep them.

Identify What's Important and What You Enjoy

Next, think about what's important to you; what you *really* want to do; what your priorities are. Here are some examples:

- Time with family.
- Time with friends.

- Maintaining or improving your physical health.
- Maintaining or strengthening your mental health.
- Time for interests and hobbies.
- Learning new skills.
- Doing some voluntary work.
- Spiritual time: time to connect with something bigger and more eternal than yourself.
- Time to do absolutely nothing. To be quiet, calm, and relax.

Which areas of your life – which health concerns, which relationships, which activities and interests – are most important to you? Think about which of these you really want to do, that you enjoy doing, and you *really* want to keep. You're aiming to have more time and energy for what makes you happy and to cut back on the things that don't.

Identify What to Let Go Of

Go back to your list of everything you typically do in a day, week, and month. How do you feel about each commitment? Be honest with yourself. Feelings of stress, anxiety, irritation, and resentment for any one commitment are telling you to let go. Maybe it's something you used to enjoy but you no longer like doing; it even annoys you; the thought of doing it makes you feel stressed.

Ask yourself:

- Do I like doing this?
- Do I want to keep doing it?
- Do I like doing it, but I don't have room for it in my life right now?

Put a line through the things that you don't like or don't want or don't have the time to keep doing. Don't forget to be honest with yourself. Crossing something out doesn't mean you're definitely going to stop doing it; at this point you're just being honest about what you do and don't want to keep doing. If you find yourself hesitating – if you feel that you 'should' keep something on the list – remind yourself that all you're doing is asking yourself these questions. For now, that's all you have to do; ask and answer the questions and keep going down the list.

Next, go back over the list and for each thing you've crossed out, ask yourself, 'On a scale of 1 to 10, how much does it matter to me?' (10 being that you're not sure and 1 being that you definitely *don't* want to keep doing it). Which commitments, tasks, or activities have you rated with a number 5 or more? What can you let go of: not do or not go to? What can you give away: delegate and get someone else to do?

If it doesn't feel good let it go, knowing that what's left is more in line with what you need and want to do with your time. You don't need to cut out everything at once – just letting go of one commitment for the foreseeable future is a good start.

Still Struggling to Let Go?

You will find that it is necessary to let things go; simply for the reason that they are heavy. So let them go, let go of them. I tie no weights to my ankles.

C. JoyBell

There are a number of reasons why you might struggle to cut a commitment. One reason might be that you find it difficult to admit that you made a mistake in signing up for something in the first place. If that's the case, you just need to know that at the time you committed yourself, you made the right choice. So yes, you agreed to be on the committee, or be part of the five-a-side football team or you paid in advance for a 12-week dance class. Now, however, you realize that it's not right for you. Perhaps your circumstances have changed, and you have new options. Maybe you've simply had a change of heart; you did enjoy being involved in whatever it was but now your feelings have changed.

That's OK! Instead of seeing yourself as fickle or unable to stick to something, think of yourself as simply having made a new decision.

Jamil, for example, realized that if he wanted to further his teaching career in adult education, a master's degree in Education would be a good thing to have. With encouragement from his manager, he enrolled on a distance learning MA course.

> After the first module – which was four months long – Jamil was struggling: 'I needed to study for about 16 hours a week and attend two weekend classes. Trying to combine the studying, my part time job and look after my young son wasn't easy but I persevered. Halfway through the second module I was totally stressed out and I had little time for my family and no time at all for friends.
>
> Eventually I quit. What I had already learnt on the course had enabled me to get a new role at work anyway, so I decided I didn't need the qualification. I certainly didn't need the stress – it was making me miserable.
>
> Rather than feel bad about quitting, I saw it as 'letting go' and I focused instead, on what I'd gained. The course was very interesting; I learnt a lot. I applied the knowledge I had already gained from the course, to my job. And, I got my life back! Less stress and more time with friends and family.'

Perhaps you don't want to lose the time, energy, or money you've already invested? Like Jamil, think about what you have to gain rather than what you have to lose by pulling out.

Whether you've put up with it for a month, a year, or even half a lifetime, you shouldn't carry on letting yourself be miserable just because you think all that past misery would be wasted otherwise. The past is in the past. Don't let the past dictate the present. Know that by continuing with something you can't or don't want to do, you will be stressed, resentful, and unbalanced. What matters is how you live your life from now on.

Unless you signed a contract – and even then, you may be able to negotiate your way out of it – there's nothing to stop you from walking away. You may feel uncomfortable – you've got to explain your change of mind to friends, family, or colleagues – but having a few uncomfortable conversations is a small price to pay for what's right for you from now on.

You can always draw something good out. At the very least, you'll have learnt something about yourself. For example, you now know that exercise classes are not for you; that to keep fit or get fitter, you're better off getting some more walking into your life; unlike exercise classes, walking is something you *do* like doing.

Perhaps, though, it's not that you can't admit you made a mistake in taking something on or you don't want to lose the time, energy, or money you've already invested. It could be that the reason you can't cut out a commitment is because you're concerned about letting other people down.

Instead of continuing under a mask of pretence, respect yourself and others enough to let them know your change of circumstance or change of heart. Have courage! Rather than focus on how anxious you feel, think of how much better you'll feel for having told the other person. Remember, having an uncomfortable conversation is a small price to pay for freeing yourself from a commitment that you have begun to resent and is making you unhappy.

Other people might need someone filling your role, but it doesn't have to be you. If you left the situation tomorrow – left the committee or the sports team for example – in three months' time what do you think will happen to those people who 'need' you? They'll adjust and quite soon, they will be fine. People can and will sort it out. But if you stay in the situation in which you feel trapped, in three months' time will *you* be fine?

You're not a bad person because you no longer want to be involved in something. Rather, you're a good person because you've recognized that something isn't right for you – that your heart isn't in it and it's time to let go. Free yourself from commitments and situations that you resent and are making you unhappy. *That* is self-care!

If you're not sure how to tell someone that you're no longer going to be involved in something, just know to be honest, clear, and succinct. Avoid waffling, rambling, or giving excuses. Don't blame someone or something else, just be honest. You only need one genuine reason for stopping doing something. Just say what you need to say. Say for example, 'I'm sorry, I'm not going to be able to continue …' Or 'Next month I'm going to stop …'

Do, though, think about what you will be willing to do, and for how long, to make it easier for the other person.

Find out their needs and accommodate them if you can, but without overly compromising yourself.

And, finally, do thank the other person or people for the opportunity to have been involved. Simply say something like:

- 'I'm grateful for the opportunity to have been doing this. Thank you.'
- 'I've learned so much from everyone. Thanks!'
- 'I've enjoyed being involved. It's been fun. Thanks!'

Say No to Others and Say Yes to Self-Care

You will, of course, need to avoid slipping back into taking on too many commitments in future. And to do this, you'll need to feel OK about saying no. This is a key skill to help free up your time and simplify your life. If you can't say no to other people, you'll find yourself taking on too much again.

There are a number of steps involved in assertively turning down other people's requests and demands for your time.

Notice how you feel. Firstly, when someone asks you to do something – to help out, to do them a favour, to get involved in something, or take something on – notice how you feel; be aware of the physical feelings. Maybe your stomach flips, you feel tension in your jaw, your heartbeat increases. Perhaps your breathing becomes more rapid and shallow and your head feels like it's tightening up. That's your body telling you don't want to do it!

Ask for more time or information. If you're not sure whether you want to agree to something, ask for more information so that you're clear what's involved. Don't be afraid to ask for time to think about it before you commit yourself. If the other person says they need an answer immediately (they have a right to do this) then rather than say yes and regret it later, it's best if you say no now.

And if someone asks you to do something, but you find it difficult to turn down the other person to their face, ask them to text or email you their request so you can get back to them. It's perfectly reasonable for you to say that you need to check your diary/calendar before you can let them know if you will or won't be able to do something. Doing this gives you time to find the right words (or the courage) with which to decline the other person's request or invitation.

Be honest, clear, and succinct. Whether it's to be a volunteer steward at a public event, to accompany a friend to the pub quiz or musical theatre, or to go canoeing – if you're going to turn down their request or invite, be clear, direct, and succinct. Simply say: 'Thanks for asking, but I'm not going to be able to do that' or 'Thanks for asking, but pub quizzes/musical theatre/ canoeing are not my thing.' Avoid waffling, rambling, or giving excuses. Don't blame someone or something else, just be honest.

Give just one reason. Naturally, the other person will want to know why. You only need one genuine reason for saying no. (Any more than one reason begins to sound like excuses.) Say, for example, 'I'm sorry, I'm not going to be able to go running with you every Sunday morning. I need the time to help my brother with his children' rather than 'I'm sorry, I would do it but I've got so much on recently; I'm up to my eyes in it at work and I can hardly think straight sometimes and now my sister-in-law is ill and my brother needs my support; I need to help look after his children. I hope you don't mind too much. Sorry.'

There doesn't, though, need to be a crisis in your life for it to be a valid reason for no longer doing something. Your reason is reason enough.

Acknowledge what the other person thinks and says but stand your ground. Once you've said what you've got to say, say no more. Just listen to the other person's response. Then acknowledge their response but stand your ground.

For example if you were deciding against the request to voluntarily run the parent and toddler group and the other person says 'But the group can't run on its own!' you could say 'I understand you need someone to run the group (acknowledging their response) but I won't be able to do it' (standing your ground).

Or, in another example, if the other person had said 'But I thought you would come with me to the gig!' you might say 'I know you were hoping I'd come with you (acknowledging their response) but I really don't like heavy metal music (standing your ground). Thanks for asking though.'

Whether you say no to people face to face, with a phone call, or by email, just aim to be honest and tell them thanks, but no thanks.

Stand your ground or negotiate and compromise. If you want to, do stand your ground. But you may also decide to negotiate or compromise with the other person. For example, you might say 'I could ask any of the other parents if they'd be prepared to run the parent and toddler group' or, in the example of not going to the gig, 'You could ask Angus or Axl to come with you to see the band. I expect they'd be pleased to be asked.'

It may take a little practice, but once you learn how to say no assertively, you'll feel more in control. If you said no more, what could you say yes to? More self-care; better mental and physical health? Allow the possibilities to inspire your 'no'; keep in mind that saying no allows you to say yes to what's important to you. It creates time and space for what matters most to you, rather than drowning in 'busyness'.

In future, reclaim your time and your wellbeing by saying no more often. Instead of automatically saying yes, get into the habit of asking yourself: 'Am I agreeing to this for me?' Start with small things, such as when you're offered a tea or coffee that you don't really want. Just say thanks, but no thanks.

Establishing Emotional Boundaries and Limits

When it comes to your commitments to other people it's not just the time and energy and practical considerations that matter. It's the drain on your mental and emotional abilities. It's easy to get caught up in the situations and emotions of those we care about, so you might also need to establish some emotional boundaries.

Emotional boundaries are the limits of your emotional abilities and involvement, in relation to other people's emotional needs and demands. Emotional boundaries are concerned with the extent that you can feel for someone else.

Having emotional boundaries protects you from being caught up in, overly involved, or manipulated by other people's emotions and problems; from accepting blame or responsibility for how someone else feels. They help you avoid, for example, feeling responsible to make up for someone's disappointments, soothe their anger, or make them happy. For example, when your partner is having a difficult time at work, it's easy to be affected by their stress and frustration. When a good friend is going through a divorce, you can get caught up in their stories about how they've felt mistreated or how their partner is being totally unfair.

Getting caught up in their situation can cause those emotions to be stirred up in yourself, especially if you relate to the situations they're talking about. And if you're currently struggling with something in your own life, now is not the time to take on someone else's emotions; it depletes the time and energy you need for yourself right now.

Establishing and maintaining emotional boundaries is not about completely turning away from someone – you can still understand and sympathize with what's happening for them and how they feel – you just don't have to be responsible. You don't have to perform some sort of emotional rescue; freeing or delivering them from their feelings.

How do you take care of yourself and avoid getting caught up in emotional rescues?

To begin with, recognize when your emotional boundaries are weak; when you drop what you're doing or need in order to accommodate their immediate emotional needs; a needy family member, for example. Or it might be when you become overly involved in someone else's emotional problems or difficulties.

Whatever someone else's emotional problems or difficulties – whether it's a friend's relationship breakup or bereavement, a colleague who is going through a disciplinary procedure at work, or a family member who's panicking because they think they're going to miss a work or study deadline or they're freaking out because they've lost their keys or phone, do avoid becoming overly involved.

Set some limits. What are you willing and unwilling to accept in terms of other people's emotional needs, demands, and behaviour? In a variety of situations, you need to know how far is too far. Of course you want to reach out and support others but there have to be limits. It doesn't mean that you should cut yourself off, but if you don't know what your limits are, how do you know if you're being helpful or interfering or just being a doormat?

Ask yourself: 'Do I feel like I just *have* to step in?' Or is it something they can do and work out for themselves? Trust other people to take responsibility for their emotional reactions and responses to their situation.

Remember, having emotional boundaries is self-care; emotional boundaries protect your wellbeing. When you notice that you're over-identifying with another person and their emotion, turn your attention back to you; take a couple of deep breaths, then visualize a line or a fence being the limit of how far you'll go. Or visualize and hear the hinges creaking as your boundary door closes.

Self-Care Actions

Identify your commitments. Write down daily, weekly, and monthly tasks, chores, activities, and commitments. Decide which things you *have* to do.

Identify what to keep. Think about what you *really* want to do and what you enjoy doing; what your priorities are.

Identify what to let go of. How do you feel about each commitment? Put a line through the things that you don't like or don't want or don't have the time to keep doing. Be honest with yourself. If you feel that you 'should' keep something on the list, tell yourself that, for now, all you have to do is ask and answer the questions: Do I like doing this? Do I want to keep doing it? Do I like doing it, but I don't have room for it in my life right now?

Next, go back over the list and for each thing you've crossed out, ask yourself, 'on a scale of 1 to 10, how much does it matter to me?' (10 being that you're not sure and 1 being that you definitely *don't* want to keep doing it). Which commitments, tasks, or activities have you rated with a number 5 or more? What can you let go of: not do or not go to? What can you give away: delegate and get someone else to do?

You don't need to cut out everything at once – just letting go of one commitment for the foreseeable future is a good start.

Let others know that you are no longer going to be involved in something. Be clear and succinct; avoid waffling, rambling, or giving excuses. Don't blame someone or something else, just be honest. You only need one genuine reason for stopping doing something.

Say no to others and say yes to self-care. Avoid slipping back into taking on too many commitments in future. Learn to feel OK about saying no.

Avoid getting overly caught up in other people's emotions. Set some limits. What are you willing and unwilling to accept in terms of other people's emotional needs, demands, and behaviour? Ask yourself: 'Do I feel like I just *have* to step in?' Or is it something they can do and work out for themselves?

5
Let Go of Friendships That Aren't Right for You

When it comes to other people, self-care isn't just saying no to their practical or emotional needs and demands. There are some people you need to say no to altogether; to cut them loose from your life. Too often we hold onto friendships that just aren't working anymore. Despite what the Spice Girls sang, it's not true that 'friendship never ends'. So why do we hold on?

Friendships are often driven by what we think of as duty; there's a sense of loyalty and we feel obliged to remain friends with some people. We feel guilty – that we're doing something wrong – if we let go. But if you're not spending a lot of time together, or you don't have much in common any more or, worse, a friend continually lets you down or puts you down, it really *is* OK to let that friendship go.

It may be, though, that you find it difficult to call quits on a friendship that's no longer right for you because you just don't know how to do it kindly and gracefully. Unfriending someone you used to know on Facebook is not the same thing as navigating your way out of a friendship face to face.

Who to Let Go

There are three types of friendship to let go of:

- Friendships where you no longer have much in common.
- Friendships that are hard work.
- Friendships that are toxic.

The friendships where you no longer have much in common are the ones where, because of a change in circumstances, the relationship is no longer beneficial to both of you. This could be, for example, a colleague, client, or neighbour. One of you leaves the job, or the neighbour moves away.

Other friendships to let go are the ones where who or what you had in common has come to an end. This could be, for example, when one or both of you leave the team, the club, the class etc. You quite literally go your separate ways. It's perfectly normal; you no longer have anything to keep you connected.

These relationships, although they were sincere and genuine, came out of convenience. But once the circumstances have changed, if maintaining the friendship is too much like hard work, it's time to let go and move on.

You *can* stop seeing old colleagues, school friends, uni friends, neighbours not with any malice but simply because you don't have the time to see them. Or the inclination. In fact, if you feel you 'ought' to rather than you want to, the friendship probably isn't going to last in a strong, connected way in any case.

The second type of friendship to let go of is the friendship that is hard work. Keeping these relationships alive can feel like pushing a piano up a hill; it's a big effort. Typically, these friendships have simply run their course. Maybe you realize you want different things; you no longer share the same interests. You've grown apart. You're bound to outgrow certain friendships. Once you're aware of that, without being unkind or feeling guilty, you can begin to let go of friendships you no longer need or enjoy; that you realize no longer fit.

What about the third type of friendship to let go of – the toxic friend? Who is this person? Toxic friends are the no-gooders whose 'friendship' is making you unhappy or miserable. Sometimes it's obvious: a so-called friend takes your money or your partner. Or they're blatantly using you – an ex-sister-in-law who is only being friends as a way of finding out what your brother – her ex-husband – is up to.

Other times it's not so obvious. We've all had friends who have gone through difficulties – addiction, relationship break-up, bereavement, financial problems. When this happens it doesn't mean that you should walk away. But if, over the months and years, you do all the emotional work – talking them down, shoring them up – 'Of course you're not to blame for what's happened in your life. Sure, let's talk about your problems. Again' – and they're never around if you need them, it's time to pull the plug.

A toxic friend:

- is rarely pleased for you when something good has happened in your life. You hesitate to tell them about something good in your life because you know they won't show that they're happy for you.
- mostly talks about themselves and rarely asks about, let alone shows interest in, you and your life.
- is only ever generous in your friendship if they are in pole position.
- allows you to initiate all the ideas, make all the plans, and be responsible for changing them if they're not convenient for them.
- is over-sensitive; your friendship is like walking on eggshells.
- puts you down or winds you up.
- competes with you.
- tries to keep you to themselves – doesn't like to share you with other friends.
- embarrasses you in front of others.
- slags you off behind your back.
- can make you doubt yourself; your opinions, ideas, and abilities.

- is only there for the good times – isn't there when you need support.
- belittles you; makes snide comments about your job, your cooking, what you wear, or how you look.
- doesn't encourage you or believe in you.
- has betrayed your trust.
- isn't loyal; doesn't stand up for you.
- is inflexible and demanding; they only want things on their terms, according to their timetable, their situation.
- tries to sell you something, or often asks to borrow money.
- keeps tabs on favours. For example 'You owe me baby-sitting because I took care of your dog'.
- reveals racist, sexist, or political views that are totally at odds with yours.
- is critical of others; constantly bitching about your mutual friends.
- you realize uses other people.
- leaves you feeling irritated and depressed.

Sure, you may have shared many of life's essentials with this person – the same class and childhood friends, holidays and hairdressers, phobias and health scares, concerns about relationships, parents, and children – but if you have a toxic friend it's time to get rid of them.

If, every time you agree to meet or chat you dread the idea of calling or seeing that person, remove them from your life!

Breaking up is not easy. Indeed, there must have been a time when you were good friends; you liked each other. But you're not a bad person because you no longer like someone. Far better, surely, to remember the good times, cut loose, and move forward.

Letting go of friends who no longer fit leaves time, energy, and resources for good friends and new friends and other things in your life. *That* is self-care!

How to End a Friendship

So while some friendships last throughout life, some make us feel like we've been sentenced for life. How do you cut yourself free?

Whether it's because you realize you can't stand seeing someone ever again, you no longer have anything in common, or you simply don't have the time for that friendship, unless you want a full-on confrontation, aim to do it gracefully with as little distress and as few hurt feelings as possible.

How to End a Friendship 1: Let it Fade Out

There's a difference between ending a friendship and letting it fade; if the friend has harmed you in some way – betrayed or hurt you in a way that can't be ignored or forgiven – then you may want to confront them or just cut them off immediately. But if the friendship has simply run its course, then let it fade. Rather than abruptly stop calling, texting, or emailing, slowly let contact diminish.

Try not returning every phone call and not initiating plans to meet up. Take your time to return texts and emails or don't return them at all. Claim to be very busy or have other excuses not to accept invitations to get together.

Saying you have a busy summer and can't fix a date, for example, will help distance you from the people you no longer want to spend time with. Try and keep your excuses as honest as possible – don't say your Mum is ill and you have to spend a lot of time with her if that's not true. But if you do have a lot going on with family members, your children, work, or travel and holidays etc. then use that as a more honest reason.

Although fading out a friendship in this way – with what can be called 'passive rejection' – avoids direct confrontation, and minimizes hurt feelings, it can take a while and requires an element of dishonesty which can feel uncomfortable. The alternative, however, is harder and harsher; 'Look, Ali, I just don't want to be your friend. I have neither the time nor the energy so I'm letting you go.'

How to End a Friendship 2: Cut the Friendship Short

If, though, you've decided that you want to break up with your friend and let them know why, don't be unkind about it. Don't dump three years' worth of resentment on their lap. If you want to explain, do it in a way that's informative rather than judgmental and overly critical. Decide in advance what you're going to say. See if you can say it in just two or three sentences. You will need to be prepared for them to react with comments about you. Simply acknowledge what they've said, then repeat what you've said and move on. For example: 'Okay, I understand that you think I've let you down and not been there for you. But I just can't listen to you talk endlessly in detail each time you get sacked or walk out of a job. Our friendship feels one-sided – you never seem to be interested in me and what's going on in my life.'

Once you've made the break, let it go. *Really* let it go.

Whether you choose to let a friendship fade out or you cut it short you might miss them now and again or look back with fond memories, but you'll find that the main feeling each time is one of relief. And, on the other side, the path is clear for you to meet new people or to spend more time with the people or the things that really matter in your life.

Refuse to be Bullied

Let go of relationships that are not working, that are hard work, or are toxic; let them fade or cut them short. If, though, another person is making you seriously unhappy, if someone's bullying you – persistently badgering, dominating, or intimidating you, continually criticizing, insulting, or humiliating you in person or online – you *must* do something. This person will not go away!

You can get help and support to deal with it (Workplace bullying: bullying.co.uk/bullying-at-work/ Cyberbullying: www.bullying.co.uk/cyberbullying/ Domestic Abuse: www.womensaid.org.uk). But you should also think about leaving; leaving the job, the neighbourhood, the relationship, or the social media account.

If you're being bullied, decide what's most important to you: surely, it's the freedom to live your life in peace? Think about the good things that can happen if you choose to leave the situation. Yes, you might have to walk away from a good job, financial stability, friends etc. but focus on the positive: that you've left the bully behind. By walking away, you put yourself in a positive position; one of being in control. You take away the opportunity for the bully to continue their behaviour. Once you've left them you can put your energy into finding a new job or somewhere to live instead of spending your energy trying to avoid, pacify, or please the bully.

The same principles apply to any situation that's making you unhappy and preventing you from getting on with your life; acknowledge what you have to lose by letting go but focus on what you have to gain. Then take the first step.

Self-Care Actions

Think if there are friendships that are no longer right for you. If you're not spending a lot of time together, or you don't have much in common any more or, worse, a friend continually lets you down or puts you down, it really *is* OK to let that friendship go.

Let it go. If a friendship has simply run its course, then let it fade. Rather than abruptly stop calling, texting, or emailing, slowly let contact diminish.

Keep it civil. If you want to break up with your friend and let them know why, don't be unkind about it; do it in a way that's informative rather than judgmental and overly critical. Do, though, be prepared for them to react with comments about you.

Refuse to be bullied. Get help and support to deal with it. Also think about leaving; leaving the job, the neighbourhood, the relationship, or the social media account.

6
Manage Overwhelm at Work

Almost everything will work again if you unplug it for a few minutes, including you.

Anne Lamott

D oes work never seems to end? Which of these situations resonate with you?

- I feel frustrated and unhappy about the time I spend at work.
- I have little or no time left to spend with friends and family, a hobby or interests.
- When I do find time to spend time with my friends and family, I feel anxious or irritable.
- Outside of work I spend time thinking or worrying about it.
- I feel tired – even exhausted – most of the time.
- I rarely get a proper break from work; a holiday, a short break, or even a day out.
- One way or another, my home and family life are suffering because of the amount of time that I'm working.

If you've got too much to do at work and you spend far too much of your days and weeks doing it, with little time for anything else you'd like to do, you have an unhealthy work–life balance.

So many of us feel overworked and stressed out, trying to balance home life and often demanding jobs. Think it's always been this way? Apparently not! Historians and anthropologists tell us that before the industrial revolution, we worked far fewer hours a week than we do today. In her book *The Overworked American: The Unexpected Decline of Leisure*, Juliet B. Schor explains that in Europe, before capitalism, 'most people did not work very long hours at all. The tempo of life was slow, even leisurely; the pace of work relaxed. Our ancestors may not have been rich, but they had an abundance of leisure. When capitalism raised their incomes, it also took away their time.'

The Trades Union Congress (TUC) believe Britain's long hours culture is having a detrimental effect on productivity and health, as the number of people now working more than 48 hours per week rises.

More people are working for longer than 48 hours per week according to research published by the TUC in April 2019. TUC General Secretary Frances O'Grady said: 'Britain's long hours culture is nothing to be proud of. It's robbing workers of a decent home life and time with their loved ones. Overwork, stress and exhaustion have become the new normal ... It's time for a change.'

A healthy work–life balance – or, to use another term; 'work–life harmony' – is about making sure that *both* your work needs and priorities and your personal needs and priorities are being met.

Of course, we don't all have the same circumstances or ambitions, constraints or strengths, and at different stages of our lives we need different things and have various demands on our time; working less when we're ill or when a family member needs support, for example, and putting in the hours when a deadline looms on a specific piece of work or we need to learn new skills or we need to earn extra money.

Some of us have a job where we work set hours and when we finish, we come home and don't give it any more thought. On the other hand, most of us have a job where it's not as straightforward as having a clear separation between work and whatever else makes up our life.

But if you're working long hours with little time for anything else, and if that carries on for too long, the cumulative effect is going to be detrimental to your well-being. Too long neglecting aspects of your life that help you resist or manage mental and physical health problems – rest, physical activity, healthy eating, leisure activities, and friendships – can leave you vulnerable.

Be Aware of How Much You Work

You can watch out for the cumulative effect of working long hours by keeping track of the hours you put in over a period of weeks or months. Each day, write down how many hours you've worked. Be aware, too, of the time you spend worrying or thinking about work when assessing your work–life balance; time spent thinking or worrying about work *is* work and a good indicator of work-related stress.

Consider whether you have let other aspects of your life slide beneath your feet – time with family and friends, time for leisure activities. Do you do less of the things you'd like or need to do than you used to, because of the time you spend working?

Take Responsibility

If you are an employee, you may be suffering from presenteeism – the practice of being present at one's place of work for more hours than are required, especially as a manifestation of insecurity about your job. You may worry that by saying something you'll put your job or career at risk. So you say nothing and suffer in silence. But you *must* take responsibility for your work–life balance.

The Mental Health Foundation recommends that 'when work demands are too high, you must speak up. This includes speaking up when work expectations and demands are too much. Employers need to be aware of where the pressures lie in order to address them.'

Take seriously the link between work-related stress and mental ill health. Creating a balance between working and not working is essential when it comes to your well-being. Sometimes it can feel like work is taking over your life. It's not just that you spend most of your day at work; even when you're not there, you're still thinking about it. And with constant access to the internet, email, and texts, it's easy to stay plugged in all day when you're at work and when you're away from it.

Cut yourself some slack. Feeling overwhelmed and over-worked doesn't mean you're incompetent and no good at your job. Don't judge yourself so harshly. Many organizations try to make do with fewer staff, so there is more work to do. But what to do if you are given more work to do when you're already stretched thin? How do you tell your manager that you simply have too much to do?

You'll need to be assertive. This means being honest, clear, and succinct. Avoid rambling or giving excuses. As calmly as you can, explain what the problem is. For example: 'This assignment requires a lot of research, which is taking up a lot of my time each day', or, 'Now that I'm managing a team, I'm spending more time planning, as well as doing my usual day-to-day work.'

Then, offer one or two ideas for addressing the issue and ask what they think. Or, ask what they'd suggest. For example: 'Which of these is most important? And how would you prioritize the rest?'

In future, don't agree on the spot to anything new if you're unsure whether you can deliver. Say, 'Tell me what you want and by when and let me figure out if I can do it based on the other work I have. I can get back to you tomorrow about it.'

Ask for Help

Give your colleagues a 'heads-up' that you're feeling swamped. If your boss won't help, they might. Perhaps they can take something off your plate or work with you on something.

It could be, though, that you think that asking for help means you're admitting you're inadequate in some way; you don't want anyone to see that you're struggling, you want people to think that you're in control and can handle things. But you get in your own way if you don't ask for help. Asking for help doesn't say something negative about you. Quite the opposite – it shows that you know that trying to do everything yourself is not the best use of your time, skills, or energy; it can leave you feeling overwhelmed and stressed and then you can't do things properly.

So, change your beliefs and expectations. Tell yourself 'I can get things done well if I ask someone else to help me.' Tell yourself that asking for help is less embarrassing than failing at whatever you're finding difficult.

Do make it easy for someone to help you, though. Ask the right person for their help – someone who has the ability, knowledge, or time. (Don't ask someone who'll make you feel stupid for asking.) Be direct – don't drop hints, sigh, or look sad. Clearly explain what you need help with. Don't waffle or apologize for needing help. Don't say 'I know you're really busy, so only if you have time … only if you want to … sorry, I know this is a lot to ask …' Talking like this implies that you don't consider yourself, your time, or the request to be valuable. Instead, simply say 'I need help with … Would you be able to … by tomorrow/the end of the week for me?' This way, the person is clear about what, how, and when to help you.

You can practise asking for help. Start small; think of things you could ask for help with in other areas of your life. Perhaps you could ask for help finding the jam in the supermarket? Help with the laundry? Walking the dog? Whatever it is, ask for help!

Work–Life Balance if You Work for Yourself

If you are an employee, and are working long hours, you can talk to your manager or HR department. But if you work for yourself, only *you* can decide a cut off point for each day. Parkinson's Law tells us that 'work expands according to the time available for its completion'. What that means is that however much time you allow yourself to spend on a task, it will end up taking that much time. So if for example, you give yourself four hours to complete a two-hour task, then the task will stretch to fill that amount of time. Give yourself half that time, completely focus on what you're doing and you're still likely to complete the task (See how to get things done in less time in 'Manage Busy, Stressful Periods at Work' on page 94).

You need to set work hours for yourself and do every-thing in your power to stick to them. Here are a few ways to switch off and leave work behind:

Set a firm cut-off time. To get yourself out of work by, say, 5 or 6 p.m. plan something; an activity or event for after work. Meeting up with a friend for a drink, a meal, a walk, to see a film etc., booking an exercise class, or stopping to make dinner. Knowing you have something else to attend to creates a different obliga-tion and moves you away from work.

Get closure; leave work at work. Before you leave work, empty your head. Simply write a note or email to your-self of any work-related things that are on your mind; tasks left to do and any concerns. Then shut the note-book, turn off your computer, and walk away.

Set boundaries. If clients or colleagues think it's OK to call you at 8 p.m., they will. Set firm boundaries around when you are, and aren't, available. If people are used to reaching you and getting a response at any time of day or night, tell them this will no longer be the case. Let them know by sending a message that says something like 'I'm changing my work hours;

from now on I won't be contactable after … p.m. but I will be available the following morning from … am.' Or, you could simply have an automatic message that replies to out-of-office emails that says something like 'Thanks for your email. My work hours are Monday to Friday, from 10 a.m. to 6 p.m. I'll reply to your message then.'

Of course, texting is based on different expectations; to send a text is to expect a rapid, even immediate, reply. But still, you need to make it clear that you're not endlessly available for work queries outside working hours. Unless it's an emergency, as long as you do answer the next working day, people get to know that and trust that they will receive a reply – but not quite as quickly as they'd hoped.

Close the door on it. If you do need to bring work home or work from home, if possible, only work in a specific room in your home so that when you're done, you can close the door on it. Unless your job specifically requires you to be on call 24/7, there's little that happens after 8 p.m. that can't wait until the morning.

Disconnect. Get used to being without your phone, tablet, or laptop. Give yourself a few hours to disconnect, otherwise you can find yourself in a state of permanent activity with little in the way of a rest or break when technology puts you somewhere that you're not. Get some fresh air. Go hiking or cycling. Play a sport. Take a phone but turn it off. Do something creative, artistic, or musical.

Avoid burnout. Whether it's stress, repeated bouts of illnesses due to a weakened immune system, or constant exhaustion, recognize the early warning signs before you start burning out. Don't ignore the signs. Your body and mind need rest to function properly. Getting support and/or taking time to recharge is crucial to sustaining motivation, perseverance, and productivity. Think of it this way: anything that increases your ability to be efficient and productive is part of your job. Anything that reduces your ability to be efficient and productive is part of your job to avoid. That's self-care!

Manage Busy, Stressful Periods at Work

Even if you're not working long hours for weeks or months on end, at one time or another you might experience really busy periods at work. At these times it's easy to feel overwhelmed and struggle to cope, to feel anxious, frustrated, and stressed. It's impossible to think clearly.

Why is that? It helps to understand what's going on in your head; to know that it's all down to two specific areas of your brain; the amygdala and the neocortex. The neocortex part of your brain is responsible for thinking, remembering, rationalizing, and reasoning. Focus and attention are primarily activities of the neocortex. The problem is that when you become stressed, the amygdala is triggered, and it overwhelms the neocortex. The amygdala in your brain is responsible for your emotions; emotions such as agitation, anxiety, frustration which, when you're under pressure, can overwhelm your neocortex and so prevent you from thinking clearly, rationally, and reasonably.

But some people thrive and rise to the challenge of lots to do; deadlines to meet, and plans to reorganize. How come? Because they just stay with what's happening and what they're doing right now. They're completely focused. They don't allow the amygdala to take over. Instead, they engage the neocortex: the thinking, reasoning part of the brain.

You can do the same. Here's how:

Accept it. Instead of letting yourself get stressed, recognize that there *is* only a certain amount of time available to get things done, or that you have to change your plans and reorganize your day. Accept it. Stop allowing the amygdala to take over and waste your time and energy railing and resenting it. Accept that the shit *has* hit the fan. If you can do that then you free up your brain to think more clearly and deliberately and you'll be more likely to find a way through.

Prioritize and plan. No matter how many times you hear it, it's still a truism; when there's lots to do and little time to do it in, you need to plan and prioritize. Work out what's really important and then work out what steps you need to take to get things done.

Write it down. Look at everything you've got to do or could be done for a particular task, for a particular day or for the week. Write it all down. Instead of letting it all swirl around your head, write it all down. Look through your list, decide what's important – what has to be done or what you really want to get done.

Set limits. Decide how much can realistically be done in an hour, a morning, a day and so on. Make some space; don't plan things close together, instead, leave room between activities and tasks. That makes your time more flexible and gives you some time in case one thing takes longer than you planned or something urgent comes up. There will always be urgent tasks that you couldn't have foreseen; you can't always predict or avoid some issues and crises. That's why, just like having savings to deal with unexpected financial issues, it's a good idea to plan for some spare time – time in your day and week to handle unexpected issues, delays, and difficulties.

Plan how you'll do it. Work out what steps you need to take to get the task or job done; know which step will follow on from the last. It's easier to get straight on to the next step if you have already planned what and how you're going to do it. It allows you to maintain a steady pace and keep the pace going.

Get help when you need it. If you need others to help, to give ideas, to solve problems with you, don't hesitate to draw them in. Is there something, or some things, that can you let go of, not do, not go to, or get some-one else to do?

Manage your energy. Take your physical and mental focus and energy into account; think about your optimum times of the day. The optimum times are the times in the day when your physical and mental energy and concentration levels are at a maximum.

Some tasks such as studying, reading or writing bids and reports, filling in forms, need all your focus and concentration. However, it's not a good use of time and energy if you try to do these things at a time of day that doesn't work for you. If you attempt a task when your mind is wandering or you're too tired to focus and you're unable to concentrate the law of diminishing returns kicks in: each minute of effort produces less and less useful results. That's because trying to get something done at your least optimum time of day takes more and more effort, energy, and concentration with the result that things end up being done badly or not at all. Conversely, getting certain things done at your most optimum time of day will take less effort and energy because it's easier to be present, to focus and concentrate on what's happening and what needs doing.

Work out the optimum amount of time you can focus on different tasks and activities. It may be that you're best doing things in short bursts, rather than one big stretch. So, that might mean that three sessions of 20 minutes' focused attention could be better than one long 60-minute slog. Try the 'short bursts' technique and see if it works for you.

Get started. Once you're clear about what you're going to do and when, get started. Do the first step. Give it your full attention. Once that one thing is done, go on to the next step. Give that your full attention too. Keep your mind focused on one step at a time. Tell yourself 'This is what I'm going to do next' and then just focus on that one step you're taking.

With this focused step-by-step approach, you can be deliberate and purposeful, not rushed and random.

You simply focus on what you're doing right now, at the present time, instead of getting stressed filling your mind with what you haven't done and what else you've got to do.

Breathe. If you *do* start thinking about what else you have to do, remind yourself you've already scheduled that in and pull yourself back to what you're doing. Pause, breathe, and pull yourself back. Tell yourself 'I have a plan. I can manage this.'

Slow down. If you find yourself speeding up, slow down whatever you do next by 25%, whether it's typing on a keyboard or digging a hole. Try slowing down by 25%. It feels strange but it really can help you to be calm, to focus on what you're doing and what's happening. Try it!

Do take some breaks. No matter how little time you have, breaks give your mind space to digest, mentally process, and assimilate what's happening, what is working and what isn't, and to decide if you need to change anything. So walk away from what you're doing and get some breathing space.

Reflect. At the end of each day take time to reflect. Ask yourself what worked today, what didn't. Do the same at the end of each week too.

Self-Care Actions

Take seriously the link between work-related stress and mental ill health. Creating a balance between working and not working is essential when it comes to your wellbeing.

Keep track of the hours you put in over a period of weeks or months. Each day, write down how many hours you've worked. Include the time you spend worrying or thinking about work. Be aware of those aspects of your life you spend less time on than you used to – time with family and friends, time for leisure activities – because of the time you spend working.

Take responsibility if you're an employee:

When work demands are too high, do speak up. But don't judge yourself so harshly; feeling overwhelmed doesn't mean you're no good at your job. Many organizations try to make do with fewer staff, so there is more work to do.

Be assertive. Be honest; as clearly and calmly as you can, explain what the problem is; what you can and cannot do. Offer one or two ideas for addressing the issue. Ask for suggestions too.

In future, don't immediately agree to do something. If you're unsure whether you can deliver, say: 'Tell me what you want and by when and let me figure out if I can do it based on the other work I have. I can get back to you tomorrow about it.'

Ask for help. Make it easy for someone to help you. Ask the right person for their help – someone who has the ability, knowledge, or time. Clearly explain what, when, and for how long you need help.

Take responsibility if you work for yourself:

Set work hours for yourself and really try to stick to them. Set a firm cut-off time. Plan something: an activity or event that you've committed to do after work. Leave work at work. Before you leave work, write down any work-related things that are on your mind; tasks left to do and any concerns. Then walk away. Set firm boundaries around when you are, and aren't, available to clients.

Manage busy, stressful periods at work:

Prioritize and plan. Decide what is and isn't a priority and then write out a step-by-step plan. Allow for time between activities and tasks. Take into account your energy levels at any one time of the day. Consider also the amount of time you can concentrate on particular tasks. If you need others to help, don't hesitate to draw them in.

Get started. Once you're clear about what you're going to do and when, get started. Keep your mind focused on one step at a time. Tell yourself, 'This is what I'm going to do next' and then just focus on the one step you're taking.

Stay in control. Breathe! Keep a steady pace and take some breaks.

Reflect. At the end of each day take time to reflect. Ask yourself what worked today, what didn't. Do the same at the end of each week too.

7
Unplug; Switch Off!

I like my new phone, my computer works just fine, my calculator is perfect, but Lord, I miss my mind!

Author Unknown

s social media harming your wellbeing? How many of the following could you answer 'yes' to?

- You feel compelled to look at social media sites every day.
- You feel frustrated with spending so much time online; you feel like you're wasting time.
- You've become obsessed with how many 'likes' you and other people get.
- You're overly concerned about your online image and keeping up appearances.
- You're replacing real life interactions with social media interactions; your partner, kids, or friends often complain they don't have your full attention because your phone is a continual distraction.

- Looking at social media makes you feel negative about yourself and your own life; you have feelings of envy and jealousy. You feel inferior to the people you follow.
- Rather than feeling connected to others, you feel disconnected; others seem happy and enjoying life and that leaves you feeling like you're missing out or doing something wrong.

I don't go on social media really. You have to be so careful not to spend your time comparing and despairing. It's so easy to do, no matter how good a place you're in. I just think if I don't see all those people then I feel like I'm in a happy, positive place, consequently I feel quite different about myself.

Yasmin Le Bon

So many studies and reports, articles and books tell us that our screen addiction – particularly the time we spend on social media – is contributing to the low-level anxiety and existential angst and frustration that define our culture of constant connection. Whether it's scrolling Twitter, Instagram, or Facebook in bed, checking emails at the dinner table, or watching videos on the train, we spend on average, one whole day a week online according to Ofcom's 'a decade of digital dependency' 2018 report.

With constant access to the internet, email, and texts, it's easy to stay plugged in all day when you're at work *and* when you're away from it. With little in the way of a rest or break from technology you can find yourself in a mode of permanent activity which always puts you somewhere that you're not. But your brain can only deal with so much incoming information at one time, and the more time you spend checking your messages, email, and social media feeds, looking at other people's lives, or posting about your own, the more 'noise' you create in your brain and the more you're overwhelming your mind.

What to do? Stop reading, listening to, and watching anything and everything? Of course not. But you *can* declutter and reduce your information consumption; you can try a 'digital detox'. You don't have to go and live in the woods and cut yourself off from the world to carry out a digital detox, but you do need at least a few days and, if possible, a week or more to take a break from your phone, your computer, your iPad, avoiding what Cal Newport – an associate professor of computer science at Georgetown University – calls 'optional digital technologies' in your life. These 'optional digital technologies' are the apps, sites, and tools delivered through a computer or mobile phone screen that you can let go of without creating real difficulties and problems in either your professional or personal life.

In his best-selling book *Digital Minimalism: On Living Better with Less Technology*, Professor Cal Newport suggests we put aside 30 days from 'optional technologies' in your life.

30 days!? Seriously?

Due to the demands of family, friends, and work, 30 days is probably not a doable amount of time for most of us to unplug completely. More likely though, you *can* start by cutting out everything for a couple of days – a couple of days when you can do other activities – over the weekend maybe? Cut out everything that isn't completely essential; what Cal Newport calls 'optional technology'.

There are three steps to a digital detox/digital decluttering.

Step One: Decide What the Limits Are

Using apps to limit screen time can be a good way to start the process of shifting your online habits. They can let you know, for example, how many times you pick a phone to use it, how much time you spend looking at a screen, and allow you to set the amount of time you do and don't spend online. Google 'apps to limit screen time' and see what app could be helpful to you.

You might decide to abstain from looking at social media or using optional technology altogether. Or you might decide to simply cut down on optional technology; to limit when and why you use technology during the digital detox.

Consider getting some support; find a like-minded friend or family member who is willing to join you in reducing screen time or social media use. If you have children and teenagers, you might make it something you all try.

It's important, though, that each of you sets their own limits for a reduction of digital technology. Your ideas and aims may be different from another person's, but the important thing is that you support each other's efforts.

Step Two: Find Other Ways to Spend Your Time

Help me back into my mind.

Pete Doherty

Whatever will you do with your time if not spending so much in front of a screen? You'll probably find it quite difficult at first and want to pick up your phone, use your laptop, iPad etc. So, this next step is crucial; *before* you abstain or reduce the time you spend looking at a screen, you'll need to think about what you'll do – other activities – instead of looking at social media, playing video games, surfing the web etc.

You might plan, for example, that before bed or in bed, instead of looking at social media you'll read a book. So do have a couple of books by a favourite author ready to read. Or you might think about some relaxation exercises you could do.

As part of the research for his book, *Digital Minimalism*, Cal Newport invited people to try the digital decluttering process. More than 1600 people signed up. One of the people in his study told him that she'd replaced browsing Reddit at night with reading library books. Another person reported listening to vinyl records from beginning to end. He discovered that the experience of listening to music is 'completely transformed when you lose the ability to tap "next"'. Someone else discovered he had more time to focus on his children. He told Cal Newport 'it felt "surreal" to be the only parent at the playground not looking down at an electronic device.'

The best way to not be in front of a media screen is simply to be somewhere else! Here are some more ideas:

Get out more: Whether it's walking, going to the gym, rock climbing, taking part in a sport or relaxing yoga, Pilates etc., get out more. Get some fresh air. Go hiking or cycling. Take a phone if you're out in the countryside on your own but turn it off.

Leave your desk at lunchtime. Unplug; switch off and go for a walk or if there's a pool near you, go for a swim. Try leaving your phone at your desk.

Stretch your mind. Learn and practise a new skill – a language, juggling, knitting. Play board games; organize game nights; play with others and be more sociable. Or do individual puzzles, crosswords, sudoku etc.

Create things. We're all creative in some way. Instead of reading about or staring at things other people create, create your own things: art, words, music, recipes, or a garden for example. Learn to do something at your local adult education centre – painting, drawing, calligraphy, photography, pottery, etc.

Meet people: Get involved! Volunteer or join 'MeetUp' groups. Instead of getting close to a screen, get close to people.

Nurture yourself. Do things you like, that make you feel good and enjoy yourself. See Chapter 14 for more on this.

Step Three: Reflect Before You Reintroduce Technology

A key aim of a digital detox is to discover the type of activities you can do that can replace time in front of a screen not just for the digital detox period, but in future too. The thing about a digital detox is that you don't just jump right back in when the detox period is at an end. That would be like going on a diet and then going back to overeating and junk food. Instead, you use the break as a launching point for changing your relationship to tech in the long term.

The real value of taking a break from technology is that it allows you to evaluate your habits and make permanent changes. So, when your break comes to an end, reflect on what you have done with the time and how you feel about it.

Before you reintroduce anything, think about what value it serves in your life.

Ask yourself:

- Does this technology provide a very real benefit; does it directly support something that I really need or want in my life?

- Is this the best way to access whatever it is I need – information, entertainment etc. – or want?
- How am I going to use this technology – apps, social media etc. – in future? In what way am I going to limit it and avoid it taking over my life again?

See if you can live with less: less social media, apps, digital games etc. None of these things are good or bad, it's what and how much you access the information they provide.

Minimize the Amount of Negative News in Your Life

People are overwhelmed and bombarded by every type of communication. You can feel like a dartboard, being hit by little shards of news – none of which is personalised or compassionate, so it can feel like a psychologically persecutory experience.

Professor Brett Kahr

We are constantly bombarded with news, real and fake, which has been shown to cause us stress.

Instead of consuming whatever is readily available, clutters your mind, and drains you, make more conscious choices about what news outlets you read, watch, and listen to. Limit the amount of negative news in your life. You're rarely better informed, your life isn't better, and you rarely feel better about yourself, other people, or the world around you for having read low-level negative information *because* you have little or no control over these events.

Steer clear of negative headlines and dire tales of what's going wrong. Look instead for uplifting stories that celebrate the best of life and be inspired by the good in the world around us. Look for stories about people that inspire you; people who have made a contribution to others; who have performed acts of kindness and compassion or who have coped admirably with adversity and bounced back.

Read the good news. Online, you can find websites dedicated to sharing inspiring and positive news from around the world: www.dailygood.org is one. There are other listed in the 'Useful Websites' section of this book.

Self-Care Actions

Try a 'digital detox'. Take a break from your phone, your computer, your iPad, and avoid 'optional digital technologies' in your life for a few days and, if possible, a week or more.

Follow the three steps: Step one: decide what the limits are. Step two: find other ways to spend your time. Step three: reflect before you reintroduce technology.

Minimize the amount of negative news – real and fake – in your life. Make a conscious choice about what news outlets you read, watch, and listen to. Instead seek out the good news.

8
Financial Self-Care

Many folks think they aren't good at earning money,
when what they don't know is how to use it.

Frank A. Clark

Money. Finance. Savings. Bank Statements. Budget-ing. What are the first things that come into your mind when you hear or read those words; what comes up for you when you think about money? Maybe you feel anxious and stressed. Perhaps you have a sense of dread. Is that because you think you're 'bad with money' and feel lost when it comes to getting your finances in order? Perhaps you avoid looking at your bank balance and you're never really sure where your money is going. You can't get to grips with budgeting and paying bills and thinking about savings; you reckon you can always deal with it later.

If you're struggling and mismanaging your finances, you may feel guilty and ashamed and think that everyone else managed to figure it out except you; you assume they're all managing their finances just fine. But whatever your financial situation, if you're finding it stressful and overwhelming, you're not alone; plenty of other people feel the same way: they're stressed, concerned, or confused with money issues. People aren't always open about money – especially when they're mismanaging it. But there are people from all sorts of backgrounds with a variety of jobs – some low paid, others well paid, and some who are very well paid – who are struggling to contend with their finances.

You might believe that simply having more money can fix your issues; all you need is an inheritance or lottery win to solve your money problems. Not necessarily so. Sorting out your money issues is a lot more to do with being able to manage money healthily, whatever the amount. In fact, if you do suddenly receive a windfall you'll definitely need to know how best to manage the money!

Just as it's important for your overall health to apply self-care to your physical, mental, emotional, and social needs, your finances need care and attention too.

Financial self-care is about both managing *and* enjoying money in a way that can help you live the life you want while staying within your means, in a way that provides for your needs and wellbeing. The aim of financial self-care is not to go from being out of control to being over-controlling. It's about being in control but being flexible and having an overall positive attitude to your money.

The good news is that there are some relatively simple steps you can take to move from negative feelings and lack of control to a positive money mindset and good financial habits.

To start with, forgive yourself for your past financial screw-ups. Few people can claim that they've never missed a credit card or bill payment, never over-spent, never indulged in impulse buys, and never dipped into their savings for something they didn't really need. You're human. Acknowledge and accept any past money mistakes then let them go and move forward.

Simple Financial Self-Care

Spend less than you earn. Probably the most obvious and only thing you need to know. Keep spending more than you earn, and you end up in a hole. It's hard to get out of the hole; you can feel that your life is dominated by trying to get out of that hole.

Make a very simple budget. The very word 'budget' can be off-putting because it brings to mind restrictions. Take a more positive outlook; be aware that limits can set you free because knowing where you're spending your money – as opposed to having no idea where it's going – is a much better place to be. It means you can tweak your outgoings: be flexible with what you spend and when. It might feel scary if you've never done a budget, but it's not hard. Write down your income, then list your bills. Use a simple spreadsheet to do the adding for you. This helps you to know what's coming in and what's going out.

Don't get into debt. If you spend less than you earn, you won't be in debt, so no problem there. Telling yourself that you can pay for it next month when you get paid is a slippery slope. If you don't have the money, go without. Use your credit card to buy something *only* if you can pay it off in full at the end of each month. Making minimum payments each month will ensure you pay the maximum interest.

Any time you feel tempted to impulse buy, take the same steps described on page 179 in Chapter 12 to avoid giving in to food cravings.

Pay yourself first. Make the savings an automatic payment that happens every payday. No matter how much or how little – £5 or £50 a week. You'll be pleased as the savings grow and especially glad when emergencies come up. There will always be crises – the boiler packs up, the car needs fixing, or there's a funeral to attend miles away.

That's all you need to know: spend less than you earn, save money, avoid debt, and pay bills on time – you're good to go. Of course, financial self-care is an ongoing process. Just as going on a crash diet doesn't really work to achieve a sustainable level of health and wellness, if your finances need sorting out you can't expect to find a quick, short fix and then go back to your old financial habits. However, establishing *good* habits is always easier said than done. So what to do?

Financial Zen; Get Financial Peace of Mind

Get yourself informed. Talk with friends and family about how they manage their money. Read about personal finances; read books and articles, listen to podcasts, and stay up to date with financial products and services.

Alice Tapper's 2019 book *Go Fund Yourself* covers five topics: Learn it, Earn it, Start it, Spend it, and Invest it. Alice says that her book covers 'all the essentials that we should have been taught at school, but weren't; from setting up a system to get you out of debt faster, to simple budgeting hacks. It also investigates the big financial challenges and opportunities we face today, … why spending no longer means owning and how being open about our finances could make us all richer.'

Enlist a financial mentor. Having someone to talk things through and suggest money solutions can be helpful. Ask someone you trust and who has sound financial judgment. It can make financial decisions less daunting, lessen the stress on you, and give you some support.

Get professional help. If your finances are a mess, think about professional help. Meeting with a financial planner can help you find solutions you might not otherwise know about.

If you can't afford a professional advisor, there are plenty of websites and books that can provide advice and ideas. The Money Advice Service www.moneyadviceservice .org.uk (soon to be the Money and Pensions Service moneyandpensionsservice.org.uk) is an organization that provides free and impartial advice on money and financial decisions. Its aim is to help anyone manage their finances as well as their circumstances allow; to provide the information and guidance people need to make effective financial decisions throughout their lives. The Citizens Advice's website – www.citizensadvice.org .uk/debt-and-money/ gives you the information you need to make appropriate financial choices including help to deal with your debt problems, how to avoid losing your home, and how to get your finances back into shape.

Self-Care Actions

Establish good, simple, financial habits: Spend less than you earn. Make a very simple budget. Pay yourself first. Avoid getting into debt.

Get yourself informed. Talk with friends and family about how they manage their money. Read about personal finances; read books and articles, listen to podcasts, and stay up to date with financial products and services.

Get advice. If your finances are in dire straits, get professional help.

PART II

Care for Your Body

9
Get Moving!

Those who think they have not time for bodily exercise will sooner or later have to find time for illness.
Edward Stanley

In comparison with previous generations, most of us are so much less active. There are a number of reasons for this. Technology, for example, has made our lives easier; machines wash our clothes and our dishes and clean our floors and carpets. We order food, clothes, and much of what we need (and don't need) from the internet and have it delivered straight to our door. We get from A to B sitting in cars, buses, and trains. And much of our entertainment involves more sitting: sitting in front of a TV or a screen.

Compared to our grandparents, fewer of us are doing manual work; most of us have jobs that involve little in the way of physical effort. Quite simply, we move around less and burn off less energy than people used to; many of us spend more than seven hours of each day sitting down, at work, on transport, or in our leisure time.

There's increasing evidence from research that sedentary behaviour – sitting down for long periods – is bad for your health. A sedentary lifestyle is thought to increase your risk of developing many chronic diseases, such as heart disease, stroke, and type 2 diabetes, as well as contributing to weight gain and obesity. In 2018, the World Health Organization listed inactivity as the fourth biggest risk factor for global adult mortality.

Previous generations were active more naturally in their day-to-day lives but today we have to make a conscious effort to integrate physical activity into our daily lives. What makes for physical activity? Anything you do that involves moving your body. It could be the activities you do as part of your normal routine: going to and from work, doing your work, walking the dog, playing with your children, housework, etc. Physical activity could also be exercise: activities you do deliberately when training or taking part in a sport that you do for competition, for enjoyment, and/or to maintain or improve your health and fitness.

Physical *and* Mental Health Benefits of Moving More

Our physical and mental health are closely linked: physical activity can be beneficial for your mental health and wellbeing too. The National Health Service website nhs.uk/livewell reports that as well as benefitting your physical health, 'research shows that physical activity can also boost self-esteem, mood, sleep quality and energy, as well as reducing your risk of stress, depression, dementia and Alzheimer's disease'. "If exercise were a pill, it would be one of the most cost-effective drugs ever invented," says Dr Nick Cavill, a health promotion consultant.'

Physical activity has an immediate beneficial effect. When you're physically active, your brain releases endorphins – the 'feel good' hormones – which can calm you, reduce feelings of anxiety and stress, and lift your mood. Exercise helps to break up racing or intrusive thoughts; being physically active can give your brain something other than your worries to focus on. And as your body tires so does your mind, leaving you less stressed and calmer.

As well as physical activity having an immediate effect, in the long term, with regular exercise, as we become fitter, our bodies can better regulate our cortisol levels. Cortisol is a 'stress hormone' that our bodies release in response to anxiety. Over prolonged periods, higher cortisol levels are not good for us! They've been linked to a wide range of health problems including heart disease, high blood pressure, a lowered immune response, as well as depression and anxiety.

As you see your body's fitness levels improve, physical activity can also help you feel better about yourself and boost your self-esteem. There are social benefits too; doing group or team activities can help you connect and enjoy being with other people.

How Much Physical Activity Should You Be Doing?

Given the evidence of how beneficial physical activity is and the detrimental effect of a sedentary lifestyle, many of us need to think seriously about how and when we can be more physically active; how we can increase the physical activities that suit our lives and our abilities and can easily be included in our day.

But just how much physical activity do you need to do? The NHS recommends that adults should do 150 minutes of moderately intense activity every week. That's roughly 30 minutes of activity on at least five days, or smaller chunks of activity spread more frequently over the week.

The NHS suggests that we need to do two types of physical activity each week: aerobic and strength exercises. Aerobic exercise and activities will help you have a healthier heart. Strength (weight-bearing) exercises will strengthen your bones and build your muscles.

The NHS website www.nhs.uk/live-well/exercise/physical-activity-guidelines-older-adults/ gives the following advice:

To stay healthy or improve health, adults need to do:

- At least 150 minutes of moderate aerobic activity such as cycling or brisk walking every week; **and**
- Strength exercises on two or more days a week that work all the major muscles (legs, hips, back, abdomen, chest, shoulders and arms).

Or:

- 75 minutes of vigorous aerobic activity such as running or a game of singles tennis every week; **and**
- Strength exercises on two or more days a week that work all the major muscles (legs, hips, back, abdomen, chest, shoulders and arms).

Or:

- A mix of moderate and vigorous aerobic activity every week – for example, 2 x 30-minute runs plus 30 minutes of brisk walking equates to 150 minutes of moderate aerobic activity; **and**
- Strength exercises on two or more days a week that work all the major muscles (legs, hips, back, abdomen, chest, shoulders and arms).

A good rule is that one minute of vigorous activity provides the same health benefits as two minutes of moderate activity.

One way to do your recommended 150 minutes of weekly physical activity is to do 30 minutes on five days every week.

What counts as moderate aerobic activity?

Examples of activities that require moderate effort for most people include:

brisk walking
riding a bike on level ground or with few hills
doubles tennis
pushing a lawn mower
hiking
skateboarding
volleyball
basketball.

Moderate activity will raise your heart rate, and make you breathe faster and feel warmer. One way to tell if you're working at a moderate level is if you can still talk, but you can't sing the words to a song.

What counts as vigorous activity?

Examples of activities that require vigorous effort for most people include:

jogging or running
swimming fast
riding a bike fast or on hills
singles tennis
football
rugby
skipping rope
hockey
aerobics

gymnastics
martial arts.

Vigorous activity makes you breathe hard and fast. If you're working at this level, you won't be able to say more than a few words without pausing for breath. In general, 75 minutes of vigorous activity can give similar health benefits to 150 minutes of moderate activity.

For a moderate to vigorous workout, try *Couch to 5K*, a nine-week running plan for beginners. www .nhs.uk/live-well/exercise/get-running-with-couch-to-5k/

What activities strengthen muscles?

Muscle-strengthening exercises are counted in repetitions and sets. A repetition is one complete movement of an activity, like a biceps curl or a sit-up. A set is a group of repetitions.

For each strength exercise, try to do:

- at least one set
- 8 to 12 repetitions in each set.

To get health benefits from strength exercises, you should do them to the point where you struggle to complete another repetition.

There are many ways you can strengthen your muscles, whether it's at home or in the gym.

Examples of muscle-strengthening activities for most people include:

lifting weights
working with resistance bands
doing exercises that use your own body weight, such as push-ups and sit-ups
heavy gardening, such as digging and shovelling
yoga
Pilates.

Try Strength and Flex, a five-week exercise plan for beginners to improve your strength and flexibility. nhs.uk/live-well/exercise/get-fit-with-strength-and-flex/

You can do activities that strengthen your muscles on the same day as your aerobic activity or on different days – whatever's best for you.

Muscle-strengthening exercises are not an aerobic activity, so you'll need to do them in addition to your 150 minutes of aerobic activity. Some vigorous activities count as both an aerobic activity and a muscle-strengthening activity. Examples include:

circuit training
aerobics
running
football
rugby
netball
hockey.

The amount and type of physical activity the NHS recommends might be beyond the reach of many of us, but even a small increase in your physical activity is better than none. If it gets your heart rate up, it counts! Just aim to start by building more activity into your daily routine and then work your way up.

Of course we've all got different levels of physical ability. But whatever your ability, you can be physically active. What's important is that you find ways to be more active that suit you and your lifestyle.

Being physically active is a lot easier if you choose an activity that you enjoy, and that fits into your daily life, your weekly routine, and your commitments. If you try to make yourself do something you don't enjoy, you're much less likely to keep it going. So, choose an exercise or sport that you enjoy. Don't feel that you have to stick at something that's not working for you. It may take a while to find something you like so do keep trying different activities. You might also find that you prefer a particular class, instructor, or group.

Work out what time you have available and find activities that fit into your day and into your week. Alternatively, drop some other commitments (see Chapter 4) so that you can make time for physical activity.

There's a wide variety of sports and physical activities you can try. The BBC's 'Get Inspired' website has lots of information about what different sports and activities

are like, and where and how to get involved. Go to bbc
.co.uk/sport/get-inspired/25416779. The NHS website
also has information about different sports and where
to find groups and classes. Go to nhs.uk/Service-Search/
Sports-and-Fitness/LocationSearch/1795.

You might want to involve a friend or family member
or join a group. Having someone to exercise with can
be a good way of making it enjoyable and keeping you
motivated. At work, you could start an office fitness
challenge: get your colleagues involved and make it a
challenge to be more active together; a walk or run at
lunchtime or a game of frisbee, football, or rounders.
Try, though, not to compare yourself with others. Just
focus on how you feel about the activity and the progress
you are making rather than what others are able to do.

Many sports are available in a walking version, such
as walking football (www.walkingfootball.com) walking hockey, or walking basketball. All across the UK,
new walking sports teams are coming together, with the
idea of getting older and less physically able individuals
together enjoying competitive team sports without the
high impact or strenuous level of activity that standard
versions of the same games require.

If you can't get out, the NHS website has lots of different routines you can follow at home; or go to YouTube
where you'll find lots of free, online exercise routines,

including everything from chair-based exercises, to yoga and cardio workouts.

If you have mobility problems, a physical condition, or find it difficult spending time out of a chair, the NHS website has activity routines you can try while sitting down and Disability Rights UK (disabilityrightsuk.org/doing-sport-differently) provides information about exercises you might be able to do. Also, take a look at bbc.co.uk/sport/get-inspired/23196217 for ideas about sports activities for people with disabilities.

There are activities you can do for free. With some comfortable footwear, walking and jogging, for example, won't cost you anything. Your local park may host a running group (Parkrun for example www.parkrun .org.uk) and anyone, regardless of their ability, can complete a weekly 5k run for free. Walking for Health www.walkingforhealth.org.uk offers free short walks somewhere near you every week. The walks are short and over easy terrain so are perfect if you're not used to being active.

Be active in nature; volunteer outdoors. The Conservation Volunteers tvc.org.uk and The Wildlife Trusts wildlifetrusts.org run outdoor volunteering projects around the UK. The Social Farms & Gardens website farmgarden.org.uk has details of community gardens and farms around the UK. And if you have a disability

and want to start or continue gardening, Thrive (thrive
.org.uk) can help.

Include More Activity in Your Day-to-Day Routine

Whether you take part in organized sports, exercise, and
activities or not, do try to build more activity naturally
into your daily routine. Here are some ideas:

- Walk, run, or cycle at least part of the way to and
  from work. If you can bike, walk, or even run to
  work, this can be an excellent way to fit more activity into your day. Even if you don't live close enough
  to your workplace to be able to do this, you can still
  find ways to make at least part of your journey more
  active. Get the train part of the way and cycle the
  rest, get off the bus a few stops early and walk, or
  park your car a kilometre or two away or find the
  furthest car park space from your workplace building to park your car. And, as much as possible, leave
  the car at home and walk the children to and from
  school.
- At work, a shopping mall, or department store take
  the stairs instead of the lift or escalator.
- If the shops are within walking distance, shop for
  food daily or every other day and carry the shopping home.

- Do more housework: vacuuming, changing the bed linen, cleaning the bathroom, cleaning windows etc.
- Do some gardening, painting, and decorating.
- Dance: put on some music while you're cooking and in between each stage of preparing your meal, dance around your kitchen.

Remember, there's no right way to get active; if it gets your heart rate up it counts.

Break Up Sitting Time

Even if you do the recommended 150 minutes of moderate aerobic exercise through the week, if you spend long periods of every day sitting down, you're still classed as 'sedentary' and at risk of health problems. How come? Well, quite simply, sitting for long periods appears to slow the metabolism – which affects our ability to regulate blood sugar and blood pressure, and break down body fat – and may cause weaker muscles and bones. If there is little muscle activity, it's as if your body is 'shutting down' when you're sitting.

The link between ill-health and sitting first emerged in the 1950s, when researchers found London bus drivers were twice as likely to have heart attacks as their bus conductor colleagues. More recently, a comprehensive review of studies on sedentary behaviour carried out by researchers from Loughborough University and the University of Leicester has linked sitting for lengthy periods with a range of health problems including an increased risk of heart disease, obesity, diabetes, and cancer.

But if sitting is the problem, could standing be the solution? Apparently not. Whether you sit or stand, it's being in one position that's the problem. So what to do? Move more; take frequent breaks that involve moving.

The UK's 2016 government publication 'Health Matters: Getting every adult active everyday' recommends that we should break up long periods of sitting time with short bouts of activity every 30 minutes. The publication suggests: 'As well as being physically active, all adults are advised to minimise the time spent being sedentary (sitting) for extended periods. Even among individuals who are active at the recommended levels, spending large amounts of time sedentary increases the risk of adverse health outcomes.' It goes on to suggest that we should reduce the amount of time we sit during our working day by taking regular time *not* sitting during work and finding ways to break up sedentary time.

As Professor David Dunstan of the Baker IDI Heart and Diabetes Institute Melbourne, Australia says: 'Breaking up sitting time engages your muscles and bones, and gives all our bodily functions a boost – a bit like revving a car's engine.'

So if your work involves sitting or standing for long periods, how you can be more active? Here are a few ideas for making your working day more active.

Set a reminder. To help you get into the habit of moving more, use an app or phone reminder to prompt you to move around for a couple of minutes every 30–60 minutes.

Walk instead of calling or emailing. Pretend it's the 1990s! Instead of emailing, texting, or messaging a colleague across the room, walk over to their desk and talk with them face to face. Put your printer and your rubbish bin on the other side of the room so you have to get up to use them. Get up and walk around while on the phone. And use the stairs, not the lift.

Turn waiting time into moving time. Waiting to use the photocopier, or for colleagues to vacate the meeting room you've booked? Don't stand there twiddling your thumbs. Take a stroll instead.

Stretch. Stand up to stretch out your chest and extend your spine to reverse the hunched position of sitting. As well as moving around, improve your posture. Activities that can help your posture include: yoga, Tai Chi, Qigong, Pilates, and the Alexander Technique.

Drink more water. But don't have a bottle by your desk so you can sip throughout the day. Instead, leave it in the staff kitchen or somewhere else so that you have to get up and walk every hour or so. Don't keep food next to you either; put it somewhere that you have to get up and go to. And use the toilets furthest away from your desk.

Volunteer for the coffee run. Go out and get your coffee, tea, or smoothie instead of letting someone else pick one up for you. Try and get in a 15-minute walk at lunch. Find a new sandwich shop that's further away from the one you usually use. And find new places to eat outside. See your lunchtime as a time to get moving and to enjoy your food, not a time to stuff something from the nearest food shop down your neck.

Organize walking meetings. Not only does it get you out of your chair, but it could be a good way to make sure meetings are more efficient and don't drag on unnecessarily.

And at home, break up long periods of sitting time with a bout of activity for one to two minutes.

Stand up and move during TV advert breaks or in between episodes if you're watching Netflix or every few chapters if you're reading.

Not everyone is able to get moving in this way if they are wheelchair users or have other mobility problems. Matthew McCarthy, a researcher at University of Leicester Department of Cardiovascular Sciences, suggests that 'completing short bursts of upper body activities using resistance bands or table-top arm cranks' may be a way to activate your muscles and get moving.

Self-Care Actions

Aim to start by building more activity into your daily routine and then work your way up. Even if you can't manage the recommended 150 minutes of moderately intense activity every week and strength exercises on two or more days a week, small increases in your physical activity is better than none.

Find something you enjoy. Look for ways to be more active that fit into your daily life, your weekly routine, and your commitments. If necessary, drop some other commitments (see Chapter 4) so that you can make time for physical activity.

Do your research. Whatever your ability, there's a wide variety of sports and physical activities you can try. The BBC Sports 'Get Inspired' website and the NHS's Sports and Fitness pages have advice and information.

Don't feel that you have to stick at something that's not working for you. It may take a while to find something you like so do keep trying different activities. You might also find that you prefer a particular class, instructor, or group.

Get support. Involve a friend or family member or join a group. Having someone to exercise with can be a good way of making it enjoyable and keeping you motivated.

Start an office fitness challenge. Get your colleagues involved and make it a challenge to be more active together.

Include more activity in your day-to-day routine. Whether you take part in organized sports, exercise, and activities or not, do try to build more activity naturally into your daily routine going to and from work, at work, shopping, and at home with household chores.

Break up sitting time. Move more; at work and at home, take frequent breaks that involve moving.

10
Go to Bed. Get to Sleep

D o you get enough sleep? Or, like so many of us, are you sleep deprived? What's keeping you up?

Just as we procrastinate when it comes to work, exercise, or other activities, it's easy to put off going to bed at night and not get the seven to nine hours the National Sleep Foundation recommends for the average adult.

Part of the problem is that the things we're doing in the evening are activities that suck us in. Our 24/7 work and entertainment culture and access to social media can all contribute to staying up later than we should. Even when you tell yourself, 'That's it, I'm going to bed at 10 p.m. tonight' 11 p.m. rolls around and somehow you're still up, watching another episode, or scrolling through Facebook, clearing up in the kitchen, or finishing off a piece of work. Before you know it, it's midnight or later. Again.

Of course, the next morning you want to feel ready to face the day head-on; instead, it feels like the day is stomping into you bedroom and pulling you from your bed. You berate yourself for not going to bed earlier as you drag yourself around all day drinking more coffee and generally feeling like crap, not to mention unproductive. And days like this don't exactly lend themselves to giving you a sunny disposition, either!

If you find that you actually want those late-night quiet hours staring at a screen, working, or faffing about in the kitchen more than you want enough sleep and a peaceful morning routine, then go ahead. But really, that's not good self-care, is it? You know it's not.

So, how can you pry yourself away from what's got a hold of you in the evening and get yourself to bed in good time?

To start with, decide how much sleep you actually need. Be aware of how you feel according to how much sleep you get. Are you raring to go after six hours or do you need eight just to function well throughout the day? Starting with the time you have to get up, work backward to find your ideal amount of sleep time.

Look at what you so often do instead of going to bed. Think about why you're doing it. Maybe you're trying to catch up with work or household chores? Whatever you need to get done, give yourself a set amount of time – 30 minutes, an hour, or two hours – to get done what you can. Then write three next steps to continue with whatever it was tomorrow. Then walk away.

Set a time to move away from a screen. You could set an alarm to remind you; set it for 30 minutes to an hour before you want to go to sleep so you have time to settle down beforehand. All of those episodes, videos, and social media posts will still be there tomorrow!

The key to getting enough sleep is to want it badly enough; to want to feel on top of things the next day. You don't need to commit yourself to a specific time to go to bed, though. Instead, create a 'bedtime window' of about an hour or so, so you're not putting pressure on yourself to get to bed exactly on time.

Go to Sleep!

If, like one in three people, you have difficulties with sleeping, reports that a lack of sleep can lead to heart disease, high blood pressure, and diabetes probably don't help you relax and get to sleep either!

But why can't you sleep? It could well be because you have a busy mind and worry, anxiety, or stressing about something is keeping you awake. Your brain keeps talking to itself; your mind is in overdrive. Thoughts and worries seem to grow and loom larger at night; you need to switch off and sleep but there's nothing to distract you from thinking about what you did or didn't do or what you have yet to face or do. And, in any case, nighttime is not usually a practical time to do anything about whatever might be worrying you.

Do's and Don'ts to Help You Sleep

If, when your head hits the pillow, thoughts buzz around in your head – what you did or didn't do joined by worries and thoughts about what does and doesn't need doing – here are some do's and don'ts that you may find helpful.

Do empty your head; write it down. If you're thinking about all of the things that you have to do the next day, write them down. Write down anything you need to remember for tomorrow before going to bed. This can help because you're externalizing your thoughts; getting them out of your head and down onto paper.

If you're worried or anxious about something, then write down one or two things you can do the next day to deal with whatever's concerning you. If, though, it's something that's already happened that you no longer have control over, rather than go over what you should or shouldn't have done or what could have happened, think instead what you've learned from the experience. Write it down. You may find that doing this makes it easier to let it go and for it to stop swirling around in your mind.

Do think positive thoughts. Instead of getting stressed thinking of what you should or shouldn't have done, or what you must, mustn't, or can't do, think positive thoughts. One way to do this is to recap the day in a positive way, before going to sleep. Reflecting on the positives in your day can shift your attention away from negative thoughts and help you to feel calmer.

Simply think of three good things that happened for you during the day. Maybe someone held a door open for you, the train arrived on time, and you received a humorous text from a friend. Perhaps you were amused to see a dog or cat chasing its own tail or you saw someone who looked like their pet. Perhaps you had a good hair day, someone else cooked dinner, and you watched something really good on TV. Or it could just be that the sun shone, you put a slice of lasagna on a plate and it stayed all together, *and* you managed to fix something: a doorknob in the house or a knot in a necklace.

Ruminating and worrying thoughts at night can hinder the process of falling asleep. On the other hand, recalling good fortune, remembering the smiles and the connections – no matter how small – that happened during the day, helps switch your mind away from going round in circles with unhelpful thoughts.

Do try a distraction. Once you're in bed, see if listening to something on the radio, or listening to music, an audio book, or a podcast distracts your mind; gives it something else to engage with.

Do establish some rituals. Getting into a bedtime routine won't necessarily make you sleepy but having a set sequence – a regular pattern – of things that you do and focus on can help calm an overactive mind.

Decide what things are most relaxing to you and that you enjoy doing at the end of the day; it may include walking the dog, having a shower or bath, reading, and/or listening to music or a podcast. Your routine could take 10–20 minutes, or it could take up to an hour or more. Whatever works for you.

Don't, though, take bedtime rituals to the extreme. It's possible to get too caught up in your prescribed routine and find yourself unable to sleep if, for example, you don't have your lavender oil diffuser with you one evening!

Don't stare at a screen. Avoid using computers, smartphones, or tablets in the two hours before you go to bed. There are four good reasons for this:

1. They stimulate your brain.
2. The 'blue' light that some devices emit can affect your internal body clock. Blue light is present in morning light so late-night gadget use can trick the body into speeding up the metabolism and making sleep more difficult. If you can't separate yourself from your phone, at least put the blue light filter on and dim the screen brightness.
3. They can be addictive, eating into even more sleep time.
4. Checking emails, the news, and social media at night can create worry and stress.

Do avoid alcohol. Although a small amount might help relax you, it can also give you a more disturbed night and disrupts dreaming.

Do move more during the day. Doing regular physical activity can help you sleep, as it makes you more physically tired.

Do try Jacobson's Relaxation Technique – also known as progressive relaxation therapy. You consciously tense and relax your muscles, one after the other, starting with your toes and working up your body, releasing tension as you go. Google Jacobson's Relaxation Technique to find out how to do it.

Don't shut your eyes. If you're lying in bed and are unable to sleep, try keeping your eyes open. As they start to close, tell yourself to resist. Often the more you try to stay awake, the sleepier you become.

Do turn the clock around so you can't see it. Fixating on the changing time is definitely not going to help you relax and fall asleep.

Don't berate yourself. When you lie there telling yourself 'I'm still awake. I'm never going to get to sleep. It's not fair. I'm going to feel horrible tomorrow, it's going to be awful' you're just creating a stress response that makes the problem worse.

Do get support. Medication such as sleeping pills and SSRI antidepressants can be helpful in dealing with short periods of severe insomnia, as they can help you break a cycle of not sleeping and return to a more regular sleep pattern.

Anxiety about sleep is just as unhelpful as anxiety about anything. Cognitive Behavioural Therapy for insomnia (CBT-I) is a type of CBT that can help you recognize and change unhelpful thought patterns and habits around sleep. Some therapists offer CBT on the NHS at GP surgeries. Your GP may also be able to refer you for CBT in your area or give you a login for an online CBT programme.

You might consider seeing a therapist privately. The British Association for Counselling and Psychotherapy (BACP), has a directory of registered and non-registered therapists. bacp.co.uk. The British Association for Behavioural and Cognitive Psychotherapies (BABCP) has a register of accredited CBT therapists. cbtregisteruk .com

Self-Care Actions

Decide how much sleep you need. Be aware of how you feel according to how much sleep you get. Starting with the time you have to get up, work backwards to find your ideal amount of sleep time.

Go to bed on time. Look at what you so often do instead of going to bed. Whatever it is – work, household chores, looking at a screen – give yourself a set amount of time. Then stop.

Don't commit yourself to a specific time to go to bed. Instead, create a 'bedtime window' of about an hour or so, so you're not putting pressure on yourself to get to bed exactly on time.

Do empty your head; write it down. If unhelpful thoughts are filling your mind – what you did or didn't do, what does and doesn't need doing, what might or might not happen – write them down so you can let them all go.

Don't tell yourself 'I can't sleep. It's not fair. I'm going to feel horrible tomorrow.' This sort of self-talk creates a stress response that makes the problem worse.

Distract your mind. Identify and reflect on the good things in your day. Listen to the radio – to music, an audio story etc. Try a relaxation technique.

Create for yourself a calm, relaxing bedtime routine.

Get professional advice and support. Talk to your doctor about the possibilities of medication or CBT to help you.

11
Feel Good. Look Good

Enjoy your body. Use it every way you can. Don't be afraid of it, or what other people think of it. It's the greatest instrument you'll ever own.

Mary Schmidt

How do you feel about your body? Are you pleased with the body you have or, for one reason or another, do you often feel disappointed that it doesn't look the way you'd like it to? Maintaining a healthy body image can be an uphill battle. It's not just the images of models and celebrities that we see on a regular basis; social media can have us believe that not only is everyone living the perfect life, they're also doing it with the perfect body! It can be hard not to compare ourselves unfavourably to the shapes and abilities of other people's bodies. We see the edited images of other people's bodies as the normal ones and we figure that ours don't match up; they're somehow 'wrong' and inadequate. But people who have what many of us would consider an ideal body are just as likely to be dissatisfied and unhappy about their looks as the rest of us.

So how can you combat a negative self-image? For a start, you can un-follow those social media accounts that make you feel bad about yourself. You can also avoid tabloid and gossip media that constantly shame celebrities' bodies. 'The eyes of others our prisons; their thoughts our cages', Virginia Woolf once wrote. She was right; you need to cut loose from the images and negative attitudes and escape with your self-esteem intact.

Reframe the Way You Think of Your Body

How can you be positive and feel more confident about your body? Certainly not by starving yourself, sweating and pummelling your body into the shape you think it 'should' be. Instead, re-frame the way you view, think, and talk about your body. For a start, shift your focus from what your body looks like to what it can do. When you think about yourself in terms of what your body can do, you start to view it in a different way. A positive way. Whatever your body's abilities or limitations, make yourself aware and appreciate all that your body can do. Every day your body is working for you: walking, running, lifting and pushing, communicating – writing, typing, and talking – hugging and holding, cutting, chopping, and stirring. And so on and so on.

Avoid getting into 'I hate my upper arms/neck/thighs/ teeth/stomach' conversations with other people. Getting caught up in a conversation about the way someone else looks, whether they've put on weight, that they think their arms are flabby, their nose is too big, their face is too lined and so on, inevitably affects the way you view your own body. Before you know it, you're falling into competitive self-criticism; as soon as your friend mentions a flaw, you trump it with one of yours. The next time a friend mentions their body hang-up, change the conversation: each come up with three body positives, for yourself and for each other. That way you can both feel better.

Look after and reward your body. Make an effort to take care of your body in the ways that you know make you feel good. For you, that might mean a great haircut, a manicure, a massage, or a relaxing bath. Whatever it is that makes you feel good about your body, do it more often. That's self-care!

Mind What You Wear; Wear it Well

I have heard with admiring submission the experience of the lady who declared that the sense of being perfectly well-dressed gives a feeling of inward tranquility which religion is powerless to bestow.

Ralph Waldo Emerson

I have a friend who says that whatever your size or shape, your body is never the problem, it's always the clothes; if something doesn't fit or look right, it's the fault of the clothes not your body. Dion Terrelonge – a chartered psychologist and trained stylist – would probably agree. Dion researches the connection between clothes and human expression; the way what we wear affects our emotions and thinking, and the way that clothes and everything related to them can serve to inhibit or assist our expression.

Dion believes that clothing is an important element of a person's wellbeing. She says: 'We've seen that exercise and physical health impact on emotional wellbeing – so do the clothes we wear.' In a 2018 interview with thepsychologist.bps.org.uk Dion describes how, after a talk she'd given, a member of the audience told Dion that she'd 'once worn her favourite David Bowie t-shirt for a week to stop a low mood from taking hold – it helped her feel happy'.

Undoubtedly, what we wear affects how we feel, and how we feel affects what we choose to wear. It's a möbius strip; a feel good/look good loop; one will feed the other. What we wear can go a long way towards helping us feel good about ourselves and boost our mood. Often, a day or situation seems to go better *because* of the clothes we were wearing; what we were wearing helped us feel more relaxed and confident.

Caring about how I present my physical self to the world makes me more present in my body. Presence in my body feeds itself, creating more care. It reminds me that I have some control over how I feel about myself.

Sally McGraw

Wearing clothes that are uncomfortable, that fight your body, that you don't feel are 'you', or that you don't really like can leave you feeling self-conscious, distracted, and irritable. Wearing clothes that are comfortable and that you enjoy wearing can help you feel so much more positive.

So wear clothes and accessories that make you look and feel good.

Start by having a clear-out. Declutter your clothes by getting rid of anything you no longer want to wear, anything that doesn't fit or make you feel good. Don't keep anything that makes you feel or look uncomfortable and self-conscious.

Simply follow the standard decluttering advice: for each item of clothing, ask yourself – do I love it? Do I like it? Do I need it? And if you're not sure whether you like it, love it, or need it, then have three categories: keep, maybe keep, and don't keep. Go through your clothes and decide what you definitely do want, don't want, and maybe want. Then go back over the 'maybe' things and decide what to definitely keep and what to let go of.

Once you've decluttered your clothes, take a new approach: no more saving things for best or shying away from clothes and outfits because you think it's not the right occasion, you're too old, too young, the wrong shape or size. If something makes you feel good and you want to wear it, wear it and start wearing it more often. And if the anecdote about the woman who wore her David Bowie t-shirt every day for a week because it helped her stay on top of things resonates with you, then do the same: wear something you love more often!

Self-Care Actions

Un-follow the social media accounts that make you feel bad about yourself. Also, avoid tabloid and gossip media that shame celebrities' bodies.

Reframe the way you think of your body. Whatever your body's abilities or limitations, make yourself aware and appreciate all that your body can do.

Change the conversation. Instead of 'I hate my upper arms/neck/thighs/ teeth/stomach' conversations with other people, talk about what you *do* like. Each come up with three body positives, for yourself and for each other.

Look after and reward your body. Make an effort to take care of your body in the ways that you know make you feel good and wear clothes and accessories that make you look and feel good.

Declutter your clothes. Clear out anything you no longer want to wear, anything that doesn't fit or make you feel good. Don't keep anything that makes you feel or look uncomfortable and self-conscious.

If you love it, then wear it! If something makes you feel good, then wear it and start wearing it more often.

12
Eat Well

E ating should be enjoyable. As the Italian opera singer Luciano Pavarotti once said 'One of the very nicest things about life is the way we must regularly stop whatever it is we are doing and devote our attention to eating.' OK, so maybe Pavarotti ate a bit too well – his weight crept up to over 20 stone.

Our bodies come in different shapes, sizes, and abilities and we have different lifestyles, but we all need to eat a varied and balanced diet that provides our bodies with what they need to function at their best. But what should you eat and what shouldn't you eat? Which new diet to follow? What are the latest must-have superfoods? What are the right foods? What are the wrong foods?

If you feel overwhelmed by all the conflicting nutrition and diet advice out there, you're not alone. Knowing what foods we 'should' and 'shouldn't' be eating can be confusing, especially when the advice seems to change regularly.

You can, though, cut through the confusion and learn how to create – and stick to – a tasty, varied, and nutritious diet that is as good for your mind as it is for your body. Of course, what makes for a diversified, balanced, and healthy diet varies for each of us depending on a number of things: a person's age, gender, lifestyle, their level of physical activity, locally available foods, and dietary customs. However, the basic principles of what constitutes a healthy diet remain the same.

There's no such thing as 'good' foods, 'superfoods', or 'clean' foods. No foods are sinful or naughty, and there's no such thing as 'cheating' with food. Healthy eating is not about diets or depriving yourself of the food you like and enjoy. The basic principles of a healthy diet involve consuming the right amount of food and drink – the nutrients you need – in the right proportions to achieve and maintain good health. Healthy eating is about feeling good, having energy, maintaining and improving your health.

For most of us, changing unhealthy eating habits is a struggle. As the cultural anthropologist Margaret Mead said, 'It is easier to change a man's religion than to change his diet.' But it doesn't have to be this way! Eating well and having a good diet doesn't have to be difficult. Instead of being concerned with counting calories and eating 'clean' foods, 'superfoods' etc., think of your diet in terms of including colour and variety, reducing processed foods, and opting for fresh ingredients as much as you can.

Shop, Prepare, and Cook

Here are some ideas for shopping, preparing, and cooking meals:

Make your kitchen accessible. Take the time to declutter and organize your cupboards, fridge, and freezer so that cooking is straightforward and relatively stress free.

Prepare more of your own meals. Cooking your own meals can help you take charge of what you're eating and better monitor what goes into your food. You'll likely eat fewer calories and avoid the chemical additives, added salt and sugar, and less healthy fats of packaged and takeout foods.

Plan quick and easy meals ahead. Planning helps. If you have a well-stocked kitchen, a few quick and easy recipes, and plenty of healthy snacks you're on the right track. Pick a few healthy recipes that you like and plan around them.

Batch cook. Cook double the amount of stews and casseroles, curries, dahls etc. Freeze the extra and you've got home-made food ready for the days you're too busy to cook a meal from scratch.

Have some meals that can be put together without going to the shops using dried goods, herbs, and spices in the cupboard and food from the freezer. A meal of wholegrain pasta with a quick tomato sauce, some defrosted prawns, or some tinned tuna, for example, could be one of your go-to meals when you are just too busy or tired to shop or cook.

'Shop the perimeter.' In general, fresh foods are found around the outer edges of most supermarkets, while the inner aisles are filled with processed and packaged foods. So, think in terms of shopping the perimeter of the store (fresh fruits and vegetables, meat and fish, whole grain breads, and dairy products), add a few things from the freezer section (frozen fruits and vegetables), and go to the aisles for spices, oils, and whole grains (like rolled oats, brown rice, wholewheat pasta).

Be aware of how you prepare and what you add to food. Avoid frying food in oil and deep-frying. Instead, sauté, steam, bake, or grill food. Try not to drown salads in too much dressing or add too much in the way of sauces – ketchup for example – to food.

You don't need to add salt to your food to eat too much of it – around 75% of the salt we eat is already in everyday foods such as bread, breakfast cereal, and ready meals. Cook with less salt. There are other ways to add flavour to your cooking without using any salt; experiment with a variety of spices and herbs.

Eat less saturated fat, sugar, and salt. Too much saturated fat can increase the amount of cholesterol in the blood, which increases your risk of developing heart disease. Regularly consuming foods and drinks high in sugar increases your risk of diabetes, obesity, and tooth decay. A diet high in salt can cause raised blood pressure, which in turn can increase your risk of heart disease and stroke.

Some packaging uses a colour-coded system that makes it easy to choose foods that are lower in sugar, salt, and fat. Look for more 'greens' and 'ambers', and fewer 'reds'.

Read the labels. Be aware of what's in your food – manufacturers often hide large amounts of sugar or unhealthy fats in packaged and processed food. It's not always easy to tell which products are healthy and which aren't. Manufacturers often have words on their packaging that make some items seem healthy when they're really full of added sugar. Common examples include labels like 'natural', 'healthy', 'low-fat', 'diet', and 'light.' While these products may be low in fat and calories, they're often full of added sugar.

Drink plenty of water. Water helps flush out the waste products and toxins from our bodies, yet many of us go through life dehydrated; this causes tiredness, low energy, headaches, and constipation (none of which put you in a good mood!). It's common to mistake thirst for hunger, so staying well hydrated will also help you avoid eating when you don't really need to. Health authorities commonly recommend you drink 8 glasses of fluid a day (where a glass holds 8 fluid ounces) which equals about 2 litres. Tea, coffee, juices, soda, and smoothies all count but be aware that these may also contain caffeine or sugar.

Eat in Moderation

For many of us, moderation means eating less than we do now. It means eating only as much food as your body needs. It means feeling satisfied at the end of a meal, but not stuffed.

Think before you eat. Take a moment to ask yourself how hungry you are on a scale of 1 to 10, and how that hunger matches up with what you've got in front of you. You don't *have* to eat everything on your plate. Excess food is just as much a waste going into your gob as it is going into the bin.

Use smaller plates. Using a 9-inch plate instead of a 12-inch plate means smaller portions. Studies have shown that food consumption is 22% lower when eating from a smaller plate.

If you go out to eat, notice how much you're eating. Eat less. Choose a starter instead of a main meal or split a dish with a friend. Reduce portion sizes of less healthy foods; you don't have to eat all of the chips; you can eat just a handful. Does that cheese on the burger really make it for you? If not, leave it out. Gravy, salad dressing, butter: you have control of how much you really need or want on there.

Try not to think of certain foods as 'wrong' or 'forbidden'. If you do that, then when you do eat them, you're more likely to feel that you've failed and berate yourself for it. Eating a sausage sandwich once a week, for example, could be considered moderation, but not five times a week!

Notice how you feel after eating. Perhaps you continue eating even after you're full – mindless of the process of eating and the sensation of being full. You can eat an entire meal, a whole sandwich or cake, and not taste more than a bite or two. Try not to eat in front of the TV or computer, while standing at the kitchen counter, or talking on the phone; it's too easy to lose track of how much you're eating.

Take your time. Slow down and be aware of food as nourishment rather than just something to stuff down your neck in between meetings or on the way to pick up the kids. Apparently, it can take your body up to 20 minutes to register the fact that you're full and during that time you may be continuing to eat. Slow down. Put your fork down every few mouthfuls. (You can even practise slowing down by swapping over your knife and fork or using chopsticks.) Check how you're feeling: 'Am I still hungry, or am I full?' If you don't feel satisfied at the end of a meal, add more vegetables or finish your meal with fruit.

Finding ways to slow down and eat and drink intentionally is part of developing a healthy relationship with food. When you take the time to enjoy your food you are more likely to notice flavours and textures and be more aware of when you are full.

Find Your Balance Across the Day

How aware are you of portion sizes? There's been plenty of information about the fact that we eat too much sugar, saturated fat, and salt, but less attention has been paid to the size of the portions on the plate. The government's Eatwell Guide nhs.uk/live-well/eat-well/the-eatwell-guide/ recommends that our diets are made up of the following:

- Fruit and vegetables: a minimum of 5 portions per day
- Starchy carbohydrates: (potatoes, bread, rice, and pasta) 3–4 portions per day
- Protein foods: beans, pulses, fish, eggs, meat, and other proteins: 2–3 portions per day
- Dairy and alternatives: 2–3 portions per day.

All very simple, but what makes for a portion? How much, for example, is a portion of pasta? The recommended portion of pasta is 75 grams.

But rather than weigh your food, a better way is to make an estimate. The British Nutrition Foundation's www.nutrition.org.uk guide provides some practical measures using your hands and spoons that can give you an idea of recommended portion sizes.

For example, one portion is:

- 2 handfuls of dried pasta shapes or rice (75g)
- A bunch of spaghetti – 75g – the size of a £1 coin, measured using your finger and thumb

- A baked potato – 220g – about the size of your fist
- About 3 handfuls of breakfast cereal (40g)
- A piece of grilled chicken breast – 120g – about half the size of your hand. (This acknowledges that bigger adults, with bigger hands, will need larger portions.)
- A piece of cheddar cheese – 30g – about the size of two thumbs together
- About 1 tablespoon of peanut butter (20g)
- About 3 teaspoons of soft cheese (30g).

Another way to estimate a portion of meat, fish, or chicken is to think of one portion as being the size of a deck of cards. A portion of potatoes would be two potatoes each the size of an egg. A serving of mashed potato, cooked rice, or pasta is about the size of a traditional light bulb.

Eat More Fruit and Vegetables

Are you eating enough fruit and vegetables? A World Health Organization review of the research into what makes for a healthy diet found that in study after study, fruit and vegetable consumption was one of the most important dietary factors associated with good health. But when, in 1990, the 'five-a-day' guidelines were published, what wasn't made clear was that five a day is not optimal for good health, it's the *minimum* amount needed to experience a significant health benefit.

But if five a day is the minimum, what *is* the optimal – the most beneficial – amount to have? Ten. Ten portions.

Five portions of fruit and veg a day is good for you, but ten is much better. A recent study – led by Imperial College London and published in 2017 – confirmed that eating ten portions – up to 800g – of fruit and vegetables was associated with a 24% reduced risk of heart disease, a 33% reduced risk of stroke, a 28% reduced risk of cardiovascular disease, a 13% reduced total risk of cancer, and a 31% reduction in premature deaths.

'Fruit and vegetables have been shown to reduce cholesterol levels, blood pressure, and to boost the health of our blood vessels and immune system,' said Dr Dagfinn Aune, lead author of the research from the School of Public Health at Imperial. 'This may be due to the complex network of nutrients they hold. For instance they contain many antioxidants, which may reduce DNA damage, and lead to a reduction in cancer risk. Most likely it is the whole package of beneficial nutrients you obtain by eating fruits and vegetables that is crucial to health,' he said. 'This is why it is important to eat whole plant foods to get the benefit, instead of taking antioxidant or vitamin supplements which have not been shown to reduce disease risk.'

The indigestible fibres found in plant foods are what the 'friendly' bacteria in your gut live off. So, increasing the amount of fruit and vegetables you eat can also increase the friendly bacteria.

The British government's Scientific Advisory Commit-tee's recommendation is for each of us to consume at least 30g of fibre each day to ensure good health. The British Nutrition Foundation followed up on this recommendation and discovered that even if you ate plenty of whole grains and nuts, you would still need to eat at least eight portions of fruit and veg each day to consume the recommended 30g of fibre. So, only eating five a day would mean missing out on a quarter of your daily fibre needs. Yet another reason to eat more than the minimum five a day!

One portion of fruit and vegetables is:

- One apple, one banana, one pear, two plums, two satsumas, two kiwi fruit, three apricots, seven strawberries, or 14 cherries.
- A slice of pineapple or melon.
- Three heaped tablespoons of fresh, canned, or frozen fruit or vegetables.
- A tablespoon of dried fruit.
- One 150ml glass of fruit juice or smoothie.
- Two broccoli spears.
- Three heaped tablespoons of cooked vegetables, such as carrots, peas, or sweetcorn.
- One and a half full-length celery sticks, a 5cm piece of cucumber, one medium tomato, or seven cherry tomatoes.
- Three heaped tablespoons of baked beans, haricot beans, kidney beans, cannelloni beans, butter beans, or chickpeas.

In the published research, Dr Aune writes: 'it is clear that a high intake of fruit and vegetables holds tremendous health benefits, and we should try to increase their intake in our diet.'

A few ways to increase your intake are:

- Add berries, a chopped banana, or a tablespoon of dried fruit, such as raisins, to your breakfast cereal
- Eat fruit – oranges, grapes, banana etc. – for a snack and/or for dessert.
- Instead of eating processed snack foods, snack on vegetables such as carrots, cherry tomatoes, cucumber, or celery along with a portion of hummus or peanut butter.
- Add a side salad to your lunch.
- Add one or two extra portions of vegetables to your dinner.

Starting today, what's one thing you could do to increase your intake of fruit or vegetables?

Manage and Take Control of Emotional Eating and Drinking

Whatever the problem is, the answer is not in the fridge.
Author unknown

Emotional eating is eating in response to emotional feelings instead of physical hunger. Many of us turn to food – usually 'comfort' or junk foods – when difficult feelings arise. It's understandable; eating is a quick way to manage your emotions. You don't like feeling stressed, sad, anxious, bored, angry, or guilty – you feel like you *need* chocolate, cake, and crisps – and so you're able to immediately comfort or distract yourself. In this way, food can feel like a friend.

But emotional eating often leads to feelings of guilt; you know that you're eating for the 'wrong' reasons; not only have you eaten badly, you feel bad too. It's a vicious circle!

The occasional spell of emotional eating is OK, but the problem is that it can become a habit, preventing you from learning how to resolve emotional distress effectively both now and in the future. Without the ability to manage feelings in helpful ways, you're susceptible not just to emotional eating, but to other unhealthy potentially harmful behaviour such as drinking, smoking, and drug taking.

Don't leave yourself vulnerable to emotional eating! Making yourself more aware of the situations, places, or feelings that lead you to reach for the comfort of food is the first step to managing emotional eating. Perhaps, for example, you let yourself get too hungry or too tired. When your body is hungry or tired, it's less able to fight off cravings or urges. So if you get too hungry, your blood sugar drops and you may feel low, tired, or irritable.

Eating regularly and choosing foods that release energy slowly – pasta, rice, oats, wholegrain bread and cereals, nuts and seeds – will help to keep your sugar levels steady. What you eat, and when you eat, can make a difference to how you feel. Avoid foods which make your blood sugar rise and fall rapidly, such as sweets, biscuits, sugary drinks, and alcohol.

You might find that instead of having a good-sized lunch and dinner, eating smaller portions spaced out more regularly throughout the day can help you maintain a more even mood throughout the day.

Emotional hunger often leads to mindless eating. Before you know it, you've eaten a whole pack of biscuits without realizing it. When you're about to reach for food, wait one minute before you eat. While you're waiting, ask yourself how and what you are feeling. Be aware of the thoughts going through your mind and what the urge physically feels like.

Overcome Cravings

Whether it's chocolate chip cookies, cheeseburger and chips, or a sausage sandwich, an occasional craving is, of course, a pleasure to indulge. Don't deny yourself those foods; limit them, but don't cut them out completely.

Why? Because when you cut out these foods completely, not only will you feel deprived and resentful, but your resentment may lead to a binge eating session of those foods when you're at a moment of willpower weakness. If you're keeping active on a regular basis, indulging yourself once in a while will not only make you happier about eating healthily most of the time, it's more likely that you'll stick with healthy eating in the long run.

If, though, you find yourself regularly struggling to fight food cravings, the good news is that you *can* overcome them. First, it's helpful to know what's going on in your brain. When you crave something, your attention has become fixated; it has focused and fixed on the crisps, chips, chocolate, or carrot cake that you want. You can think of nothing else and a compelling momentum develops: a combination of thinking about the crisps, chocolate etc. as well as feeling a physical sensation.

With cravings, you focus on the desirable qualities of what you want, while ignoring the downside – the undesirable aspects or consequences of having given in to the craving again. So what to do? To begin with, acknowledge the craving. Recognize it as an urge, without trying to change it or get rid of it. Be aware of thoughts going through your mind and what the urge physically feels like. You can even name it in your head: 'Look at that, an urge to eat chocolate.'

Then, take these three steps:

1. Loosen the fixation. Remind yourself of your good intentions. This helps to keep you focused on what matters most and can get you through the moments when your impulses try to take over.
2. Surf the urge. Imagine the urge as a wave in the ocean. It will build in intensity, but soon break and dissolve.

Imagine yourself riding the wave, not fighting it but also not giving in to it. Know that cravings aren't permanent, they come and then they go. Just like the waves.

3. Distract your mind. Deliberately bring your attention to something that will help to divert your mind – something you know will engage you. Phone a friend for a chat. Do something physical – go for a brisk walk, wash up, vacuum, sweep the path.

Find other ways to comfort yourself besides food. Sure, these other ways will not always be as quick and easy at comforting you as food. But a shower, a good book or film, yoga, a run or a walk, a chat with a friend about how you're feeling are all better for your wellbeing.

Be careful about the foods you keep at hand. It's more challenging to avoid urges and cravings if you have less healthy foods at the ready. Keep healthy food readily available; stock up your fridge with small batches of fresh fruits and vegetables. At work, store small quantities of nuts and dried fruit and berries in a jar.

Set Yourself Up for Success

In the book *Harry Potter and the Goblet of Fire*, Dumbledore says to the students at Hogwarts: 'there will be a time when we must choose between what is easy and what is right.' When it comes to eating well and healthily, you *can* aim to do both.

Taking care of yourself by eating healthily is simply a matter of making the healthy choices easier to choose and eat. As with increasing the amount of physical activity in your life, the best approach is to make a few small changes at a time. Make easy changes. The first step might be, for example, adding a salad to your diet once a day for the first two weeks. You could also replace some drinks with water as opposed to soda. Or begin by eating more vegetables with two meals for one week. Or you could eat a healthier breakfast. In fact, if you do that – change your breakfast – you've changed one third of your meals!

Be realistic and specific about what changes you could make. You're far more likely to succeed with a healthier diet if you start with small, easy changes that you can accommodate than try a sudden drastic change and end up feeling deprived, resentful, and ready to give up. As each small positive adjustment becomes established, you can continue to add more healthy changes.

Self-Care Actions

Teach yourself to eat well. Learn how to create – and stick to – a tasty, varied, and nutritious diet that's as good for your mind as it is for your body.

Think of your diet in terms of including colour and variety, reducing processed foods, and opting for more fresh ingredients as much as you can.

'Shop the perimeter.' Think in terms of shopping the perimeter of the store: fresh fruits and vegetables, meat and fish, wholegrain breads, and dairy products. Read the labels on packaged and processed food.

Prepare more of your own meals. Plan quick and easy meals ahead.

Think before you eat. Be mindful of what, when, and how much you're eating.

Eat in moderation. Learn what makes for the recommended portions of different foods.

Eat more fruit and vegetables. Five portions of fruit and veg a day is good for you, but ten is much better.

Don't leave yourself vulnerable to emotional eating. Don't, for example, let yourself get too hungry or too tired.

Overcome food cravings and urges. Remind yourself of your good intentions. Surf the urge; allow the urge to pass. Distract your mind; do something – anything that distracts your mind from the urge or craving.

Set yourself up for success. Make the healthy choices easier to choose and eat. Make a few small changes at a time. Make easy changes.

13
Be Drink Aware and Stop Smoking

I s your drinking healthy?

Many of us drink too much without realizing it. Drinking too much could be having a detrimental effect on you both now and in the future; alcohol overuse is linked to mental health problems, liver disease, 7 forms of cancer and more.

For each of us, the recommended safe limit of alcohol is 14 units a week. Fourteen units of alcohol is equivalent to six pints of average-strength beer or 10 small glasses of low-strength wine. If you regularly drink more than 14 units a week or the effects of alcohol are having a negative impact on your life, it's time to consider reducing how much and how often you drink.

If you cut down, you may find that the immediate effects include feeling better in the mornings and being less tired and having more energy during the day. Drinking can affect your sleep; although it may help you fall asleep quickly, it can disrupt your sleep patterns and stop you sleeping well; even just a few drinks can interfere with the normal sleep process. So cutting down on alcohol should help you feel more rested when you wake up.

Hangovers can make you feel anxious and low. If you already feel anxious or depressed, drinking can make this worse, so cutting down may put you in a better mood generally.

As well as the short-term effects, there are other, long-term benefits to reducing the amount of alcohol you drink. Many alcohol-related health risks don't appear until later in life. Drinking less will reduce your risk of developing serious health issues such as cancer and liver or heart disease and could contribute to lowering your blood pressure. You may not be able to see the effects of cutting back, but you *will* be making a positive difference to your long-term health.

Drinking less can also have a positive impact on other aspects of your life including your relationships and work. Drinking can affect your judgement and behaviour. You may behave irrationally or aggressively when you're drunk. So reduce your drinking and you reduce the possibility of acting like a dick.

And, of course, you'll save money. Whatever you spend on alcohol in an average week, multiply this by 52 and you'll have your spend for the year. If you were to set this aside every month, you could save up towards something you really want.

Writing for the *Guardian* in July 2019, Gay Alcorn described her experience of giving up alcohol for a month.

> [What I found with] giving up alcohol for a month is that it's ridiculously, unexpectedly good. I had entirely novel experiences. Like meeting friends for a drink before the theatre and not drinking. Like not drinking on a Friday night. Like going to a family lunch and sipping mineral water. Like going to a book launch and standing around for an hour without drinking the warm, cheap white wine.
>
> … After two weeks or so, I posted on my Facebook page: 'Have discovered (a bit of a surprise to be honest), am a better, kinder, more present, more energetic, more productive, happier person when I don't drink. What a bummer!' I was only going to give up for one month but these things were hard to dismiss. I was more mentally available for friends and family, a better listener, less swift to judge. I was more productive, and the stir of ambition returned. I ate better, exercised more. I slept like a baby, no longer waking up feeling foggy. I was a happier person.
>
> … Alcohol is a toxic, addictive substance that our body works hard to expel. That's it. I'm not preaching but it's the truth and we all kind of know it. But after one month, the benefits of sobriety outweighed the benefits of alcohol, no matter how hard I tried to spin it.

Of course, for many people, drinking in moderation can add to life's enjoyment; a pint of good quality beer in a pub with friends, a cold bottle of cider on a hot day, a glass of red wine with an enjoyable meal in a restaurant, a glass of champagne to celebrate a special occasion. But for other people, drinking in moderation isn't easy.

To cut down on alcohol successfully you need to adopt steps that can be put into practice no matter where you are. You can find tips on cutting down at nhs.uk/live-well/alcohol-support/tips-on-cutting-down-alcohol.

Drinkaware drinkaware.co.uk and Alcohol Change alcholchange.org.uk are charities working to reduce alcohol misuse and harm in the UK. Their websites have information to help people make better choices about drinking. They are not anti-alcohol; they're about alcohol change, enabling people to be more likely to drink as a conscious choice, not a default.

Stop Smoking

Do you smoke? Haven't stopped yet? It's never too soon. And it's never too late!

Think About the Health Benefits

The most immediate benefits are:

Heart risks reduced. Quitting can lower your blood pressure and heart rate almost immediately. Your risk of a heart attack declines within 24 hours.

Lung damage reduced. Within two weeks of quitting, you may notice that it's easier to walk up the stairs or uphill because you may be less short of breath. The cilia in your lungs – which work to keep the airways clear of mucus and dirt, allowing you to breathe easily and help to fight off colds and infection – start to regrow and regain normal function very quickly after you quit smoking.

Lower cancer risk. Quitting smoking will lower your risk of getting cancer. Quitting smoking will prevent new DNA damage from happening and can even help repair the damage that has already been done.

Stronger immune system. When you quit smoking, your immune system will become stronger.

Stronger muscles and bones. You'll increase the availability of oxygen in your blood, and your muscles will become stronger and healthier.

And, as well as better health, you'll enjoy life more as a non-smoker: you'll have more money and a cleaner environment.

Prepare to quit. You're more likely to be successful in your attempts to quit smoking if you plan ahead. Start by setting a date to quit. Pick a time when you aren't too stressed or have other stuff going on in your life. You might find it easier to quit smoking when you're away from your normal routine; on holiday, for example.

Get support. It can be hard to change a long-term habit, but you don't have to do it on your own. With support from friends, family, and professionals, you're more likely to be successful. Go to nhs.uk/smokefree for information, support, and advice. You'll find information on this website about your local Stop Smoking Service with provides free expert advice, support, and encouragement to help you stop smoking for good. Research shows that you're up to four times more likely to quit successfully with their help.

You can also join Facebook groups and forums where people are actively helping each other to quit smoking. These are a good place to connect with others who are going through or have been through the same experience. You can talk with them, learn from them, and use their experience to quit for good.

Get help from medication. Nicotine replacement therapy (NRT) can double your chances of success; as well as nicotine patches, there are tablets, lozenges, gum, and a nasal spray. It's much better, though, to use stop smoking medication along with intensive support, such as group or one-to-one support, than to use medication alone.

Consider CBT or hypnotherapy. Hypnotherapy is a popular option that has helped many smokers to quit. Choose a hypnotherapist with a healthcare background, such as a doctor, psychologist, or counsellor. Check they're registered with an organization that's accredited by the Professional Standards Authority.

Cognitive Behavioural Therapy (CBT) is the process of restructuring your thought processes and combining this with new learning behaviours to quit smoking. Go to cbtregisteruk.com to find a CBT therapist who is registered with the British Association for Behavioural and Cognitive Psychotherapies (BABCP).

Read about it. *Allen Carr's Easy Way to Stop Smoking* is a bestseller and many people have stopped smoking for good after having read his book.

Whether you intend to cut back or to quit completely, if you do relapse just start again. Don't let a setback make you give up! Instead, try and identify why it happened. What can you learn from that? What will you do differently from now on?

A relapse doesn't mean you're right back where you started. Typically, you'll take two steps forward and one step backward: making progress then losing ground, learning from mistakes and using what you have learnt, to move forward.

Be patient and kind to yourself; don't think of difficulties as failure, but instead think of setbacks as part of the process of change; opportunities to learn, to do better next time.

> ## Self-Care Actions
>
> **Make yourself aware of how much you drink.** If you regularly drink more than 14 units a week, reduce how much and how often you drink.
>
> **Remind yourself of the benefits.** As well as the short-term and long-term health benefits, there are other advantages to reducing the amount of alcohol you drink. Drinking less can also have a positive

impact on your behaviour and your judgements, your relationships and work. And you'll save money.

Get advice and support. You can find tips on cutting down on the NHS, Drink Aware, and Alcohol Change websites.

Stop smoking. It's never too soon. And it's never too late!

Remind yourself of the health benefits. Reduced risks of heart and lung damage, a lower cancer risk, stronger immune system, stronger muscles and bones.

Prepare to quit. You're more likely to be successful in your attempts to quit smoking if you plan ahead.

Get advice and support. With support from friends, family, and professionals you're more likely to be successful. Go to nhs.uk/smokefree for information, support, and advice.

Don't give up giving up! Don't let a setback make you give up! Instead, try and identify why it happened. What can you learn from that? What will you do differently from now on?

PART III

Care for the Good Times and the Bad Times

14
Be with Good People and Do Nice Things

As the first few lines of Benjamin Zephaniah's poem 'People Need People' tells us:

> People need people,
>
> To walk to
>
> To talk to
>
> To cry and rely on,
>
> People will always need people.
>
> To love and to miss
>
> To hug and to kiss.

Human beings are social beings; we need to interact with others; to connect and to feel that we belong and are valued. Having relationships with others is important; we need *positive* relationships. Who are the positive people in your life? Who do you enjoy spending time with? Who, for example, makes you laugh; is fun and lively to be with? Is there someone with whom you have shared interests? Who in your life is supportive and encouraging?

The positive people in your life do not just have to be friends or family; they could be colleagues or neighbours. The person you can talk to if you're worried could be your GP, a counsellor, someone at a support group or at the end of a helpline. Maybe the person who introduces you to new worlds, ideas, and interests is a tutor on a course or an author of interesting books. Maybe it's someone on TV – David Attenborough and his programmes about wildlife or Brian Cox and his programmes about space, for instance. Perhaps there's a comedian on radio or TV who makes you laugh. Choosing to surround yourself with people who uplift you is a form of self-care.

As Karl Marx advises; 'Surround yourself with people who make you happy. People who make you laugh, who help you when you're in need. People who genuinely care. They are the ones worth keeping in your life. Everyone else is just passing through.'

Connect with friends and family. Show interest, care, and concern. Keeping regular contact in person is good but even a message or phone call can make a difference. Of course, having good relationships with others isn't something that just happens. You have to make time and effort.

If you don't have good friends and family around you – if you need more positive relationships in your life – start to meet new people. Think of the things you like to do, such as singing or gardening, playing or watching a sport – and find people who share the same interests. Of course, making new friends isn't always easy. But just as keeping friends takes time and effort, so does making new friends; you need to be willing to meet others, to be yourself and give something of yourself. You *can* make new friends, but you can't sit and wait for other people to come to you. You need to get out there!

Have a look at www.meetup.com. The website enables people to find and join groups of other people in their local area who share each other's interests. There are groups to fit a wide range of interests and hobbies, plus others you'll never have thought of. There are book groups, art groups, film and theatre groups, and sci fi groups. Hiking and running groups, football groups, netball groups, and cycling groups.

People who go to 'Meetups' do so knowing they'll be meeting others who are also open to making new friends. If you find people who are just as keen on, for example, board games, Nordic walking, or craft beers as you are, then you'll find it relatively easy to connect and make friends with them. And when you're doing something that's fun and meaningful, your ability to form connections will come naturally.

Volunteer

Another way to connect with other people and experience positive relationships is through volunteering for a cause or local community initiative that interests you. Doing something to benefit someone else can make you and the person you are helping feel good. Studies show that helping others creates feelings and attitudes that can lead to better physical health, better mental health, and overall happiness.

Volunteering is also a good way to meet people – other volunteers – and make friends. You can meet and create bonds with people who want to make a contribution to the lives of others; you have a common cause that is another opportunity to create meaning and purpose in your life.

Volunteers can do almost anything: there's a huge range of volunteer opportunities available to you. Whether it's serving tea at a local hospice, helping at a local community food project or an animal rescue centre, working with refugees, advocating for someone with a learning disability or mental health problem, or mentoring people leaving the criminal justice system, not only can you make a contribution to other people's lives, but you can be involved in something that's relevant to your values and interests. It could be something related to politics, the environment and conservation, arts and music, or perhaps some voluntary work with older people, families, and children. See the 'Do It' website www.do-it.org for volunteering opportunities in the UK.

Find Spirituality

The positivity and sense of connection that can be gained from helping other people is also a key aspect of spirituality.

We all have some sort of image in our minds when we hear the word 'spirituality'; maybe you see a group of monks living a simple life in a faraway place. Perhaps it's an image of someone wandering down a mythological spiritual path on their 'spiritual journey'. But quite simply, spirituality is a sense of being connected and being part of something bigger, more eternal than both the physical and yourself. You don't have to be religious in order to be spiritual. Even if you regard yourself as an agnostic or atheist, you can feel a sense of connection from contemplating a beautiful sunset, or the power of the sea, or the daffodils appearing, once again, in your garden in Spring.

Spirituality helps you to feel grounded in the present and yet connected to the past and the future. You can choose to define what spirituality is for yourself. Your own sense of spirituality can be experienced by anything from cheering your team along with ten thousand other people, to something as quiet and simple as gazing at the enormity of a star-filled sky.

Raise your awareness; think about what you *already* do that makes you feel connected. Perhaps it's playing a team sport, singing in a choir, gardening or being outside with nature, or being with thousands of others at a music festival. Get connected: appreciate the beauty of what we are naturally a part of, concepts such as music and art, wildlife, and the miracles of nature.

Do More of What You Enjoy; Small Pleasures and Awesome Things

When you recover or discover something that nourishes your soul and brings joy, care enough about yourself to make room for it in your life.

Jean Shinoda Bolen

In Chapter 10 you'll have read about how identifying and reflecting on the positive events that occurred during your day can be conducive to helping calm your mind and help you fall asleep. Not only does identifying and reflecting on positive events encourage a positive mindset, but it raises your awareness of the little things that bring you pleasure.

What, for you, makes for small pleasures? A bubble bath, a hot shower, warm towels? Fresh clean sheets? A book by one of your favourite authors, singing along to music in the car and/or car dancing? Maybe, on a cold morning, it's putting on an item of clothing that's been sitting on a hot radiator? What about a lie-in? A kiss, a cuddle, or holding hands? Perhaps it's an open fire, sitting in the sun, or a walk in the rain? Maybe talking to your dog or cat is one of your small pleasures?

A friend of mine starts their day by watching an episode of the American sitcom 'Cheers' or the US version of 'The Office' every morning. They say it gets their day off to a good start. You could do the same; start your day with an episode of a favourite sitcom or podcast.

Get into the habit of identifying and indulging in small pleasures: the ordinary and the extraordinary, the familiar and the new, the small things and the bigger things. The cheap and the expensive, the easily accessible, and the things that require effort.

Find 'Flow'

As well as the small moments of pleasure, do things that engage and absorb you for longer periods of time.

Think of the times you've been so engrossed in what you were doing that time passed without you realizing. It could have been a book, a film, or a piece of music that absorbed you. Perhaps it was a game, a musical instrument, or a sport you were playing. Maybe it was singing in a choir or dancing to music. Whatever it was, as you did it, no other thoughts entered your mind because you were completely focused and engaged in what you were doing; you didn't even notice the time that was passing.

When you're doing something that keeps you effortlessly focused and engaged like this, you're experiencing something known as 'flow'. When you're in a state of flow, it's as if a current of water is effortlessly carrying you along. Your awareness merges with what you're doing, and you are completely 'in the moment'. Your thoughts are positive and in tune with what you're doing.

What do you like doing? What activities can you engage with for half an hour, or immerse yourself in for an hour or more? Swimming? Running? Playing or watching football? Maybe you enjoy cooking? Singing? Fishing? Playing guitar? Perhaps it's something you do on your own – meditating, reading, sketching, gardening – or with other people – team sports, board and computer games, singing in a choir, running?

Identify the things you enjoy doing: hobbies, sports, interests. Know that when you need to bring together your mind, body, and environment they are activities where you can easily experience flow.

Get Out in Nature

A 2019 study by the University of Exeter Medical School has found that people who spend at least 120 minutes a week in nature are significantly more likely to report good health and higher psychological wellbeing than those who don't. The study reports that it doesn't matter whether the 120 minutes is achieved in a single visit or over several shorter visits, and is not limited by gender, age, occupation, ethnicity, socioeconomic background, or whether the person had a long-term illness or disability.

Try and organize your days so that you can spend time in nature. Most people have somewhere near them, even if it's only a small park or garden. With more than 62,000 urban green spaces in Great Britain, one should never be too far away. The Wildlife Trusts www.wildlifetrusts .org have a searchable online map of their nature reserves, almost all of which have free entry; they also provide a list of accessible nature reserves. And Ordnance Survey's Greenspace – getoutside.ordnancesurvey .co.uk/greenspaces/ shows thousands of green spaces for leisure and recreation.

Do Awesome Things

And as well as small pleasures and periods of flow, plan for bigger things to look forward to. Whether it's a day or a night out with friends, a weekend away, a holiday, or an adventure, get something booked and put into your diary or calendar. Even if it's weeks or months from now. Then, whenever you need a shot of happiness, remind yourself about it.

Self-Care Actions

Identify who the positive people in your life are. Spend more time with them; 'Surround yourself with people who make you happy. People who make you laugh, who help you when you're in need. People who genuinely care.'

Meet new people. If you need more positive relation-ships in your life, find people who share the same interests: leisure pursuits, hobbies, and voluntary initiatives.

Find spirituality. Get a sense of being connected and being part of something bigger, more eternal than both the physical and yourself. Spirituality helps you to feel grounded in the present and yet connected to the past and the future.

Identify and indulge yourself in small pleasures. The ordinary and the extraordinary, the familiar and the new, the small things and the bigger things. The cheap and the expensive, the easily accessible, and the things that require effort.

Find 'Flow'. As well as the small moments of pleasure, do things that engage and absorb you for half an hour, an hour, or longer.

Get out in nature. Spend time outside in green spaces – a garden, a park, or the countryside.

Do awesome things. As well as small pleasures and periods of flow, plan for bigger things to look forward to: days out, short breaks, a holiday, an adventure.

15
Self-Care When Life Is Really Difficult

When you come to the end of your rope, tie a knot and hang on.

Franklin D. Roosevelt

In Chapter 2 you will have read about the importance of self-acceptance; acknowledging and accepting your failings and foibles and not letting your shortcomings define you or undermine your worth and bring you down. What, though, if you're facing something more serious than having screwed up, made a mistake, or failed to achieve something?

Perhaps, for example, you recently lost something or someone you love: you've experienced a bereavement or a relationship breakup, or a close friend or family member has moved away. Maybe you have financial problems and you're worried about money. Perhaps you've lost your home or your job. Or your home has suffered a flood or fire.

Maybe you've moved somewhere new and very different and you're struggling to adjust. Maybe you've become a parent for the first time and you're finding it difficult to cope. Or it could be that there was something you desperately wanted – a child, a qualification, a place on the team, or a promotion – but didn't get? Perhaps someone else has badly let you down, betrayed your trust, or cheated on you?

Any of these things can knock you sideways and leave you feeling sad and lonely, anxious and vulnerable. Caring long term for someone else – a child, your partner, a sibling or parent – with a physical or mental illness, or coping with your own physical or mental illness, can be enormously challenging. So can incidents of discrimination, abuse, or being bullied. Perhaps someone you really care about – your partner, parent, or child – is struggling with a problem and it's having a serious effect on you too. (Someone once told me that you're only as happy as your unhappiest child. It's true.)

Understanding Sadness

Whatever the issue and the circumstances, when you're going through the kind of event that overwhelms you or even devastates you, it helps to understand what's going on. It may be hard to believe, but feelings of sadness and disappointment, shock, or grief are there for a good reason. Like all 'negative' emotions, sadness, disappointment, shock, and grief do have a positive intent. What's the positive intent? It's to slow down your mind and body to give you time to take in the new circumstances and accept that what has happened *has* happened. Nothing can change that.

You'll probably go over events and ask yourself 'What if ...?' 'Why didn't I ...?' and 'I should have/they should have ...' 'I wish I hadn't ...'. Thoughts like these are part of the process of facing what has happened or is happening.

It *is* OK to be sad and upset. You might think, 'I shouldn't be so upset. What's wrong with me?' but you need to accept sadness for what it is: a temporary and useful state that can help you adjust – to get used to changed, different circumstances – and to accommodate the changes and learn to live with them.

You may feel disconnected and disorientated. As the author C.S. Lewis noted after the death of his wife, 'At times it feels like being mildly drunk, or concussed. There is a sort of invisible blanket between the world and me. I find it hard to take in what anyone says.'

Whether you've been bereaved or suffered some other loss or major life change, now really is the time for self-care. Be kind to yourself; don't expect too much of yourself, your mind needs time to catch up with and process the changes in your life, your new reality.

Sadness also conveys to others that you are experiencing loss or failure so that they can respond appropriately – with kindness and compassion – give you time and space, comfort and support you. So treat yourself like a good friend – with the same care and kindness. Let yourself be sad.

Take the Pressure Off

When you're going through a tough period in your life, you need to let go of some of your commitments and obligations so that you can slow down and adjust. Ask yourself which of your commitments and obligations are not so important right now? Ask yourself questions such as:

- What do I want to do with my time?
- For now, what do I *have* to do and not have to do?
- Where do I want to go and not go?
- Who do I want to see and not want to see?
- Who depends on me – who do I have to see?
- For now, what and who can I drop?

In 2013, for the website tinybuddha.com Maria Moraco wrote about how she coped after the death of a parent, the breakdown of a committed relationship, and the death of a pet:

> I handled it okay. Just okay. I'm not sure it was a time to expect myself to be amazing. One of the biggest lessons I learned going through those experiences was that I really had no idea how to take care of myself.
>
> When I was going through these experiences, I assumed that having coffee or drinks with a good friend would

help me feel better. Normally, I really enjoy this and find it relaxing.

Surprisingly, I found I was not enjoying these get-togethers. It wasn't that my friends weren't sympathetic. It was simply that I needed me (and me alone) time to process and heal. The very greatest friend simply could not offer me what I could offer myself at that time. We're all different. Some of us will find great comfort in surrounding ourselves with friends; others will benefit from immersing ourselves in our hobbies or in our work. There's no right answer here. It's a matter of paying attention to our own needs and what works for us, not what general opinion says that we need.

This is also not a time to cave to social or family obligations if we don't find them to be nourishing. If the weekly family dinner is fun and supportive, go for it. If it's more of a 'dredging up the past' fest, then let that routine go until you're feeling stronger.

In times of stress, compassion for self, in the manner that is the most soothing and fulfilling for us, is a priority. To be present in our lives, and for our loved ones, and yes, for ourselves, this self-care is imperative.

In response to Maria's post, a reader wrote;

… when I was looking after my parents who both got diagnosed with cancer … everything I read and everyone I spoke to said 'you must look after yourself', you must eat right and exercise and go for walks. It was all about things that I should do – but at the time I was already doing more than I was actually capable of and looking after myself just seemed to add more stress to an already stress filled life.

I wish someone could have told me about all the things that I didn't have to do and didn't have to feel guilty about letting go of. Don't worry about cleaning your house – take a bubble bath instead. Don't worry about visiting the in-laws, send your husband on his own (it is his family after all) and stay home and read a good book. Stop feeling like you have to do it all or feel guilty if you let someone down! Focus on the important situation at hand and let everything else go (at least for a while) stop beating yourself up!

When you're going through a really difficult period, then like Maria and her respondent, take the pressure off. There are times in your life when you don't have to cope brilliantly and you don't have to be amazing; you just need to do the minimum to get by, because that's all you *can* do and for now, that's just how it's going to be.

The advice in Chapter 4 concerning reducing your commitments definitely applies here. Cutting back on commitments doesn't mean that you should remove yourself from everything and everyone, but in tough, difficult periods of your life, self-care requires you to be aware of your limits and stick to them; saying 'no thanks' or 'not now' to requests for your time; for your presence, abilities, and contributions.

When you're feeling overwhelmed, it *is* OK to say no. It's not selfish or unkind. When someone asks you to do something, makes a suggestion, or extends a well-meaning invitation notice, how do you immediately feel? Disinterested? Anxious? Pressured? Stressed? Simply say, 'Thank you for asking me, but I don't want to/can't/ don't feel up to it …'

There's no need for a long explanation and excuses. Be honest; you only need one valid reason why you can't or don't want to do something.

However, although you may need to step back from life for a while when you're going through a difficult period, don't drop all your connections with others. Your link to family and friends is important for your sense of well-being and belonging. You just need to tighten the circle for a bit and limit your time to spending it with those people who support or comfort you in some way.

It's easy to feel like few people, if any, care or understand what you're going through. Often, other people don't know what to do or say so they do or say nothing. So, even though you're the one who's facing a tough time you may need to be the one to get in touch.

Reach out to those you can trust; friends or family who will listen and comfort, who have a calm concern and won't try to judge or fix you. You might want to tell them how you've been feeling – confused, anxious, sad, angry, upset, exhausted – but if you find that some friends can't handle your feelings that's OK. Everyone has their abilities and their limits. If a friend or family member is not able to listen or talk with you about how you're feeling, ask them to do something practical to help. Leave talking about how you feel till you are with someone who *is* able to listen and talk with you about it. And whatever it is other people are able to do for you, do tell them you appreciate their concern or support.

You may want to talk to someone you know who has experienced the same difficulties. But if you don't know of anyone who's gone through the same experience, you can Google a local support group or helpline. You'll be able to talk to people who understand what you're going through, provide opportunities to share experiences with others that have been or are going through the same thing – a mental or physical illness, coping with an off-the-rails teenager, being a carer for someone else, a relationship breakup, bereavement, redundancy, financial problems etc. – and get information and ideas on how to cope, to move on, or feel better.

You can also read about how other people have coped; there are others who've made it through and then written books about how you can do it too. Take advantage of their knowledge and experience and get some insight; read blogs and books written by people who've been where you are.

If, though, you've no one to talk to or feel that a helpline or support group isn't helpful, if you feel overwhelmed too often or for too long, then *do* go and speak with your doctor.

Indulge Yourself with Comfort, Reassurance, and Small Pleasures

When life is very difficult you need to do what you can to make things easier. To a greater or lesser extent, you need to be self-indulgent. Self-indulgence isn't a bad thing; it allows you to create conditions that enable you to integrate what's happening – or has happened – into your life.

It's hard to look forward to each day when you know you will be experiencing pain and sadness. So each day decide to have something to look forward to. No matter how small it is, have something you can do that you enjoy. Whether it's reading, baking, going for a walk, having lunch with a friend, singing – in a choir or on your own – gardening, doing a crossword, playing computer games – do whatever it is that you like to do.

Comfort yourself. Think of pleasant things you can do. Get a massage. Eat comfort food. Wear a favourite piece of clothing. Have a warm bath or a hot shower. Hug or cuddle someone who loves you. Holding hands or walking arm in arm with a friend or family member can comfort and reassure you.

Do something nice for someone else; a small kindness that will take your mind off what you're going through.

Watch an uplifting film. Or funny pet videos on YouTube. Look at a book or website with beautiful scenery or beautiful art. Whatever brings you moments of pleasure.

Listen to music. Music can help you access a range of feelings: anger, sadness, and happiness. Music can soothe or uplift you. Music that you find beautiful and uplifting can provide hope and encouragement – Flaming Lips

'Do you realise' for example, or Elbow's 'One day like this' or for something more upbeat – Mark Ronson's 'Uptown Funk' or Fleetwood Mac's 'Don't stop thinking about tomorrow' and Primal Scream's 'Moving on up now'. These are just songs which came immediately to my mind; of course, you'll have your own favourites from one or many genres of music – classical, jazz, country or folk, reggae, R&B and so on.

If you play an instrument or sing, then play that instrument or sing. If you have a hobby or passion that you can 'lose yourself' in, it can help you to feel engaged and connected. Whatever it is that you get comfort and enjoyment from, make yourself do it. Do something that gives you pleasure and comfort each and every day.

Doing things that you enjoy can help you move through sadness and difficulties, even if you don't initially feel like doing them.

There isn't one right way to take care of and be kind to yourself when you've been through a really difficult experience. When times are tough, what works for you might be different for what works for someone else. And what works for you today might be different from what helped a month ago or in a few months' time. Nothing stays the same – part of taking care of yourself is to be flexible. Again, treat yourself as you would treat someone else – a friend or loved one – who'd suffered a loss or serious change in their life.

Moving On

At some point, how sad, angry, upset etc. you feel now will become a sad memory. When you're ready, you can work towards that. What if it feels like nothing is ever going to change; that you won't be able to move on? The thing is, things *do* change, and you *will* move on but not until you decide that you *want* to move forward and you *are* going to move on.

Positive change starts with hope. Hope encourages you to believe that things will eventually improve and be good and that you will feel better.

Hope is not a switch you can simply turn on, but hope *is* something you can create. It's within your control to become more hopeful; you have the ability to generate your own hope. How? Well, rather than dwell on what's past and what is out of your control – which makes you feel hopeless – you start thinking about what you *can* control. And that helps you feel hopeful. You take small steps to build your hope up every day by working on the things you do have some control over.

It helps if you can set some small goals for yourself. In an article for the *Telegraph* newspaper's *Stella* magazine in 2017, journalist Victoria Young wrote that, after the trauma and sadness of six miscarriages, 'it began to dawn on me that I just had to stop waiting to feel better'.

She realized that grief can make you self-centred and that she'd become absorbed in her own little world.

Victoria made a list of steps towards action she might take over the next year.

> I found ways to start thinking about other people. I began volunteering for events at my son's school. I booked afternoons off work to take an elderly friend for a pedicure. When the same friend got ill, I committed to regular visits. I helped out at a community fair ... I started exercising ... I did something physical every day; walking 10,000 steps, classes in the park, running with mums from the school and sometimes, freezing dips in the Ladies Pond on Hampstead Heath. The physical effects were good but mentally it was my salvation that no matter how sad or bad I felt, my mood was elevated by doing something physical that forced me into the moment; away from thought.

> To combat isolation, I joined a book group. I'd always dismissed such activities as not for me but I needed company. Forced out of my comfort zone of solitude I found that regularly getting together with other women, some of whom I didn't know, was cheering. I also enrolled in a fiction writing class. Getting lost in other people's lives and tragedies was a great distraction from my own.

> I bought a sewing machine, joined a sewing a class, and made curtains and cushion covers. Tapping into my creativity made me feel very gently happy.

Victoria says she had always been curious about mindfulness, so she did an eight-week course. She found that focusing on the moment was 'a colossal relief'. She also did yoga – she found that she benefited from just being in her body, in the moment, for an hour or two each week – and some counselling; 'Over the course of a year, therapy helped me celebrate the many things I have instead of rueing those I don't.'

Victoria says she realized that 'you don't get over this kind of grief; it's more like a work in progress'. Although time alone hasn't healed her, she recognizes that the things she'd done to help her try and feel better have helped the sadness fade:

> For the longest time I couldn't imagine feeling anything other than bleak, sad and despairing. Then one day, out of the blue, I did. As a result, this new year, I feel more full of hope and happiness than I ever thought possible.

Although Victoria says that things changed 'out of the blue' it's likely that it was *because* she made changes – positive changes – that gave her control, provided distractions, comfort and small pleasures – that she was able to feel a lot less bleak, sad, and despairing.

You can do the same: decide that you *are* going to take control and move forward; start making small changes that will help begin a shift in your life and give you hope and help you move on. Like Victoria, be open to new ideas and ways of doing things. Think of something or some things you can do – small steps you can take that will enable you to move forward to a brighter future. This is your starting point.

Have patience though; take things one step at a time; try to avoid rushing into things. Sometimes, in an effort to move forward, it's easy to make rash decisions; rush back to work, move home or jobs, break ties with people in your life, or take on new relationships too quickly.

Let Go and Move On

Start making small changes that will help start a shift in your life and help you move on.

You might like to keep an 'achievement journal'. Note the things, no matter how small, you achieved that day. When you're going through a difficult time in your life and are struggling to feel better, noting small achievements will help you to see that you can do things and you can build on those things to help you move on.

What gets included may depend on how you're feeling that day. Sometimes it might simply be that you got out of bed and got dressed. It might have been an effort to get out of bed and it was an achievement worth nothing down. Sometimes it might be household chores or work tasks. There's a wide variety of things in our lives that make for small achievements. Maybe, for example, you sent an email to enquire about something, had a chat on the phone with friend, read a couple of chapters in a book, made a new recipe, listened to the news, cleaned the bathroom. Maybe today was the day you went out with friends for the first time in ages or you booked a holiday. Perhaps you returned to work.

Regularly write in an achievement journal and every now and then you'll be able to look back through your journal to reflect on all that you've learned and achieved. It will all add up to quite a lot of small achievements.

You can also include those things that you feel grateful for – the things you appreciate. Look for the positives. When life feels like it's weighing you down more than normal, it can seem like everything is wrong, bad, or hopeless; there's nothing positive. Even during the worst of times, there can be something to be thankful for. Every day, there is something positive and good. Most of the time it's not obvious. You have to look and, often, you have to look hard. In Chapters 10 and 14 you will have read about the idea that, at the end of each day, you identify and reflect on three positive things that happened in your day. It need only to be the small things – this morning's coffee, hearing birds sing in your garden, a funny text from a friend, something good on TV – or it could be the bigger things. Maybe you have a good job, or a supportive boss, family, partner, neighbour, or friend. Whatever – add them to the achievement journal.

Expect to have bad days, though. Weeks, months, a year or more after a difficult time in your life, you might have days when, although it felt like there was no reason at all to feel knocked back, you just did. If you're having a bad day, especially if it's after a period of better days, there's no need to wonder 'What's wrong with me?' Bad days do happen. They will pass. Accept that sometimes you can have a bad day for an obvious reason or for no apparent reason. On those days, be kind and gentle with yourself. Phone a friend, stay in and eat pizza and have an early night. Or whatever works for you.

As the Austrian poet Rainer Maria Rilke said, 'Let everything happen to you: beauty and terror. Just keep going. No feeling is final.'

If, however, you're concerned that you're not able to move forward, ask for help. You might want to talk through the things you're finding challenging with a trained professional. Talking therapies can help with many difficult life problems – from coping with traumatic experiences and events, to dealing with depression and anxiety, or managing harmful emotions and behaviours.

Ask your GP for advice about seeing a therapist or counsellor or find an accredited therapist at the British Association for Counselling and Psychotherapy (BACP) at www.bacp.co.uk.

Self-Care When You're Ill or Injured

None of us chooses to get injured or be ill. But, to a certain extent, we *can* choose how we deal with it.

Having an injury or being ill is *the* time to prioritize self-care – to be gentle and easy with yourself – so don't pressure yourself to carry on as normal. If you work, call in sick. If you have social plans, cancel or reschedule. If there's housework to do, leave it. Rest is more important. Feel guilty? It's misplaced guilt; you're not doing anything wrong by doing what you can to get better. Time and energy you put into other things are time and energy diverted from you getting better. Your health is important and in the long run you will be able to do more if you rest now, as it will speed up your recovery.

Any day that you're unwell, make sure you're comfortable. Wear comfy, loose clothes, curl up in bed or bring your duvet and pillows into the living room and make yourself comfortable on the sofa. Gather everything you need – medication, tissues, books and magazines, laptop and phone and their chargers, the TV remote, and anything else you may need or want – into one place so you don't have to keep expending energy and effort getting up and down.

Being unwell is a time to do things that bring comfort and calm. Simple things like a hot water bottle or a long hot bath. Re-read a favourite book or something new by a favourite author. Use this opportunity to catch up on some reading or that film or series you've been meaning to watch. All of the little pleasures that you usually don't find time for can be enjoyed when you're unwell. There's nothing to feel guilty about – you're not doing anything wrong by indulging yourself in this way. Quite the opposite – you're doing everything right; you're taking care of yourself so that you can get better.

Eat healthily but do also eat comfort food – soups and stews, hot buttered toast, pizza, macaroni cheese, hot chocolate – whatever you love. Don't let food shopping sap your energy, though. Try to plan for everything you're likely to need for the next few days and either ask someone else to get it or do an online food order.

If you have children to take care of, know that you can't be Supermum or Superdad while you're feeling ill. Your children certainly won't hold it against you forever if you ditch the sports practice, craft activities, and outdoor adventures for a few days and let them resort to the TV and computer games, will they? Give yourself – and them – a break.

And in the evening, when the children go to bed, if you're not already there, go to bed too. Don't use the evenings to get other stuff done. Your body imposes a curfew when you're ill – obey it or it will punish you the next day!

Let Others Take Care of You

Let others know that you're unwell. Don't be boring and go on about it but don't say you're fine when you're not. Don't say you don't want to be any trouble. Don't be a banana! Take help when it's offered. And if someone says, 'Let me know if I can do anything', think of something!

If they don't offer, then ask. Ask for help and support. Be specific about what it is that you'd like someone to do for you and ask them. Whether it's getting the washing off the line, walking the dog every day, making some phone calls on your behalf, or just keeping you company for a while, let others help. Just as being ill is an opportunity to do things that bring you comfort, it's also a time to ask for and accept the care and help of others. So if someone you trust is happy to help, just let them. Even if they don't do things exactly how you'd want them, let go of perfection and accept that right now, how and what they're doing is good enough.

If your illness is chronic – it occurs regularly – then plan ahead for a crisis. When you're really unwell, it can be hard to ask for the support you need or figure out what help you want. Making a crisis plan while you're well can help you feel you have some control and that you've already thought about and can let other people know how best to help.

Ease Back into Your Life

As you start to feel better, it can be tempting to throw yourself back into your usual routine. But pushing yourself to take two steps forward could mean you then find yourself going three steps back. If you've been physically unwell or injured, even if you feel better, your body will be weak from the illness and your immune system needs to regain its strength. Know that energy you use up doing everyday things is energy diverted from getting better. Be kind to your body. Have patience, take it slowly, one step at a time.

Illness makes us slow down, so when you're getting back on your feet, you need to do simple things. Things that don't take up too much time and energy. Write a letter or email to someone you haven't caught up with in a while, go through old photos, declutter a cupboard or a shelf, or just clear your coat pockets or bag of receipts, train tickets etc. Small, simple tasks can seem like a chore when you're in the midst of a busy life, but when you're unwell those little tasks might provide the simplicity and just the right pace for you and won't take much energy either.

You might also use the time to respond to the gestures of kindness from others – phone calls, emails, letters to reply to.

Use the change of pace that illness or an injury brings to reflect on what you want to do when you do feel better. Sometimes, it's possible to trace back your illness to an imbalance in your life. Maybe you've been pushing yourself too hard, at work or in your family life? Maybe you've been overdoing it with junk food, alcohol, smoking, or drugs? Maybe you've not been getting enough sleep or exercise? Maybe you sustained an injury because you were rushing or taking short cuts with something?

Too often, when we tip the balance we risk being overwhelmed and then fall ill or get injured. Illness and injury can be a wake-up call – to value your health and redress the balance; to take care of yourself.

Self-Care Actions

- **Let yourself be sad.** See sadness for what it is: a temporary and useful state that can help you adjust – to get used to changed, different circumstances – and to accommodate the changes and learn to live with them.
- **Take the pressure off.** Reduce your commitments. In difficult periods of your life, self-care means being aware of your limits and, for now, sticking to them; saying 'no thanks' or 'not now' to requests for your time; for your presence, abilities, and contributions.
- **Don't drop *all* your connections with others.** Your link to family and friends is important for your sense of wellbeing and belonging. Reach out to those you can trust; friends or family who will listen and comfort, who have a calm concern and won't try to judge or fix you.
- **Google a relevant support group and/or helpline.** You'll be able to talk to people who understand what you're going through, provide opportunities to share experiences and ideas on how to move on or feel better.
- **Ask for practical help.** If a friend or family member isn't able to listen or talk with you about how you're feeling, ask them to do something practical to help. Leave talking about how you feel until you are with someone who *is* able to

listen and talk; to offer comfort, sympathy and reassurance.

- **Have something to look forward to each day.** No matter how small it is, have something you can do that you enjoy and brings you small comforts.
- **When you're ready to move forward, be open to new ideas and ways of doing things.** Think along the lines of 'It might help to ...' or 'I might try ...' or 'I could ...', or 'Now I'm going to ...'. But be careful not to rush into things.
- **Try keeping an 'achievement journal'.** Note the things, no matter how small, you achieved that day. You can also add those things that you feel grateful for – the things you appreciate.
- **Expect to still have bad days.** They will pass. On those days, be kind and gentle with yourself.
- **Any day that you're unwell, do simple things that bring comfort and calm.** Take help when it's offered. If others don't offer, then ask. Be clear and specific about what it is that you'd like someone to do for you and then ask them. Even when you feel better, your body will be weak from the illness and your immune system needs to regain its strength. Know that energy you use up doing everyday things is energy diverted from getting better. Be kind to your body. Have patience, take it slowly, one step at a time.

Websites and Books

Health Quiz

www.nhs.uk/oneyou This NHS website has an online quiz to help you assess how healthy your lifestyle is.

Health Apps

nhs.uk/apps-library/ The NHS Apps Library can help you find trusted health and wellbeing apps. Health apps can be great for learning more about health issues and enabling people to apply self-care; to manage and improve your health. The apps are assessed against a range of NHS standards.

Pharmacies

nhs.uk/using-the-nhs/nhs-services/pharmacies/ Make use of your pharmacist. You can talk to a pharmacist instead of your doctor for advice regarding a specific minor illness or injury. Go to this websites to find out more about the services and support pharmacies can provide.

Mental Health Advice and Information

mentalhealth.org.uk The Mental Health Foundation aim to help people to thrive through understanding, protecting, and sustaining their mental health.

mind.org.uk 'Mind' offers information and advice to people with mental health problems.

elefriends.org.uk Elefriends is a supportive online community from the mental health charity Mind.

verywellmind.com Very Well Mind is a US website offering advice and information on a range of mental health issues.

Counselling, Psychotherapy, and Cognitive Behavioural Therapy

bacp.co.uk The British Association for Counselling and Psychotherapy (BACP) has a directory of registered and non-registered therapists.

cbtregisteruk.com The British Association for Behavioural and Cognitive Psychotherapists (BABCP), has a register of accredited CBT therapists.

Workplace Issues

acas.org.uk ACAS offers advice and information on a wide range of workplace issues to try and help employees and employers to solve their problems at work. You can ask a question on their online helpline or phone them on 0300 123 1100.

tuc.org.uk The TUC (Trades Union Congress) aim to make the working world a better place for everyone.

Managing Bullying

For help and advice to deal with:

Bullying at work: bullying.co.uk/bullying-at-work/

Cyberbullying: www.bullying.co.uk/cyberbullying/

Domestic abuse: www.womensaid.org.uk

Good News

These websites report positive, uplifting news stories:

theguardian.com/world/series/the-upside

huffingtonpost.com/good-news/

goodnewsnetwork.org/

positivenews.org.uk

Financial Advice

The Money Advice Service and Citizens Advice provide free and impartial advice on money and financial problems and issues. issues.moneyadviceservice.org.uk (soon to be the Money and Pensions Service moneyand pensionsservice.org.uk) and citizensadvice.org.uk.

Food and Nutrition

The NHS's Live Well website has advice and information on eating well and being a healthy weight. nhs.uk/live-well/

The British Nutrition Foundation provides information on food and nutrition; to make nutrition science accessible to all. nutrition.org.uk

Physical Activity and Exercise

The BBC's Get Inspired website has lots of information about what different sports and activities are like, where and how to get involved. bbc.co.uk/sport/get-inspired/25416779

The NHS website also has information about different sports and where to find groups and classes. nhs.uk/ Service-Search/Sports-and-Fitness/LocationSearch/1795

If you identify as female, the This Girl Can website has ideas, from trying a new sport to being more active as part of your day-to-day life. thisgirlcan.co.uk/

Disability Rights UK disabilityrightsuk.org/doing-sport-differently provides information about exercise for anyone with a disability and BBC's Get Inspired website has ideas about sports activities for people with disabilities. bbc.co.uk/sport/get-inspired/23196217

Parkrun – to find out about local 5k running at a park near you, go to parkrun.org.uk

Walking for Health offers free short walks somewhere near you every week. walkingforhealth.org.uk

The Conservation Volunteers tvc.org.uk and The Wildlife Trusts wildlifetrusts.org run outdoor volunteering projects around the UK.

Ordnance Survey's Greenspace – getoutside.ordnance survey.co.uk/greenspaces/ shows thousands of green spaces for leisure and recreation.

The Social Farms & Gardens website farmgarden.org.uk has details of community gardens and farms around the UK. If you have a disability and want to start or continue gardening, Thrive can help. thrive.org.uk

Men's Health

The Men's Health Forum's mission to improve the health of men and boys in England, Wales, and Scotland. menshealthforum.org.uk

Dealing with Substance Misuse

The NHS defines substance abuse or misuse as 'the continued misuse of any mind-altering substance that severely affects a person's physical and mental health, social situation and responsibilities'. Whether it's drugs, alcohol, nicotine, or solvents – any of these substances may give you a temporary feeling of wellbeing or of being in control – but all of them can ultimately damage your health.

If you feel you have a substance misuse problem, you can seek help and advice from your GP. If you'd rather not talk with your GP, you can approach your local drug treatment service yourself. Visit the FRANK website talktofrank.co.uk or call the FRANK drugs helpline on 0300 123 6600 to find local drug treatment services.

Drinkaware drinkaware.co.uk and Alcohol Change alcholchange.org.uk are charities working to reduce alcohol misuse and harm in the UK. Their websites have information to help people make better choices about drinking.

Stop smoking! Go to nhs.uk/smokefree for information, support, and advice. You'll find information on this website about your local Stop Smoking Service. You can also phone the NHS Smokefree helpline on 0300 123 1044.

Social Groups for Leisure Interests, Hobbies, and Learning

Find and join groups of people in your local area who share your interests. There are groups to fit a wide range of interests and hobbies, plus others you'll never have thought of. www.meetup.com

Volunteering

Visit the Do It website www.do-it.org for volunteering opportunities in the UK.

Books

Digital Minimalism: On Living Better with Less Technology by Cal Newport

How to Break Up With Your Phone: The 30-Day Plan to Take Your Life Back by Catherine Price

Go Fund Yourself; What Money Means in the 21st Century, How to be Good at it and Live Your Best Life by Alice Tapper

Breaking Free from Emotional Eating by Geneen Roth

The Body Image Workbook by Thomas Cash

Allen Carr's Easy Way to Stop Smoking: Read this book and you'll never smoke a cigarette again by Allen Carr

About the Author

Gill Hasson is a careers coach, has over 20 years' experience in the areas of personal and career development, and is a freelance tutor/teacher in mental health issues for mental health organizations. She also teaches and delivers training for adult education organizations, voluntary and business organizations, and the public sector.

Index

abuse, bullying as 80–1, 233
acceptance and commitment approach
    25–6
achievement journal 222–3
achievements 44–5
advice, sources of 120, 231–7
aerobic activity 128, 129, 130–1, 132
alcohol consumption, reducing 185–8
Alcorn, Gay, giving up alcohol 187
amygdala 94–5
anxiety
   about sleep 152
   physical activity reducing 127
assertiveness, saying no to others 62–6
Aune, Dr Dagfinn, fruit and vegetables
    174, 175–6

bad days, accepting 223–4
balanced diet 165–6
bedtime rituals 149–50
blood sugar levels 177–8
body image 157–8
   reframing 158–9
boundaries
   emotional 66–8
   hours available for work 92–3
brain areas 94–5
budgeting 117–18
bullying 80–1, 233
burnout, avoiding 93–4

cancer 34, 174, 189
Carr, Allen, stopping smoking 191
Cavill, Dr Nick, exercise benefits 127
Citizens Advice 120, 234

clothes
   decluttering 161–2
   and wellbeing 159–61
Cognitive Behavioural Therapy (CBT)
    152, 190, 232
commitments
   being overwhelmed with 51–3
   cutting back on 214
   disengaging with 53–4
   identifying 54–6
   letting go of 56–62
community volunteering 135–6, 200
comparison with others 31–5
compliments, accepting 45–6
cooking 167–8
cortisol 127
counselling 152, 190, 224, 232
cravings for food, overcoming 178–80
creativity 47, 108
critical thoughts *see* negative thoughts

debt 118, 120
decluttering
   digital 106–10
   your clothes 161
diet 165–6
   fruit and vegetables 173–4
   government recommendations 172–4
   recommended portion sizes 172–3
difficult times
   moving forward 219–24
   taking the pressure off 212–16
'digital detox' 105–10
Digital Minimalism (Newport)
    105–106, 107–108
disability 135, 235

241

Index

Index

Index